Mercedes Benz

Buyer's Guide

Roadsters, Coupes, and Convertibles

Fred Larimer

MOTORBOOKS
INTERNATIONAL

First published in 2004 by Motorbooks International, an imprint of MBI Publishing Company, Galtier Plaza, Suite 200, 380 Jackson Street, St. Paul, MN 55101-3885 USA

Motorbooks International titles are also available at discounts in bulk quantity for industrial or sales-promotional use. For details write to Special Sales Manager at Motorbooks International Wholesalers & Distributors, Galtier Plaza, Suite 200, 380 Jackson Street, St. Paul, MN 55101-3885 USA.

ISBN 0-7603-1811-5

Editorial: Peter Bodensteiner and Amy Glaser
Design: LeAnn Kuhlmann
Printed in China

About the Author:

Fred Larimer grew up in car-crazy southern California during the 1950s and 1960s. His interest in all things automotive started early on with visits to Ascot Speedway and Lions Associated Drag Strip. During the late 1960s his interest in German and British sports cars began when he attended several Times Grand Prix and USRRC races at Riverside International Raceway. Fred and his wife Pamela reside in Orange County, California.

The pictures for this book were photographed with Nikon cameras and lenses using Fuji Provia F100 film.

Contents

Preface 4

Acknowledgments 5

Introduction 6

Chapter 1   W113 230SL/250SL/280SL: 1963–1971 Basic History 16

Chapter 2   W107 350SL 4.5 450SL/380SL 560SL—1971–1989 Basic History . . .30

Chapter 3   R129 SLs: 1990–2002 Basic History 50

Chapter 4   R170 SLK230/SLK320/SLK32 AMG: 1998–2004 Basic History 66

Chapter 5   W111/112: 1960–1972 Basic History 80

Chapter 6   W114 250C/280C: 1969–1976 Basic History 92

Chapter 7   W123 280CE/300CD: 1978–1985 Basic History 102

Chapter 8   W203 C230 Kompressor/C320 Sport Coupe:
2002 on Basic History 110

Chapter 9   W124 300CE/E320: 1988–1995 Basic History 120

Chapter 10   W208 CLK320/CLK430/CLK55 AMG: 1998–2003* Basic History 130

Chapter 11   W126—380SEC/500SEC/560SEC: 1982–1991 Basic History 144

Chapter 12   W140 Coupes: 1993–1999 500SEC/S500/CL500/
600SEC/S600/CL600 Basic History 154

Chapter 13   W215 CL500/CL55 AMG/CL600: 2000 on Basic History 162

Chapter 14   Rare and Collectible MBs 300SL Gullwing and Roadsters:
1954–1963 Basic History 176

Appendices   One 188

Two 190

Index 191

Preface

I have been familiar with Mercedes-Benz automobiles since I was a preteenager. My grandfather brought me back a miniature replica of the W196 streamliner from one of his business trips to Germany in the mid-1950s, and the Gullwing has always been one of my favorites. Mercedes-Benz cars have always stood out to me as well-engineered and mechanically sophisticated. As I researched material for this book, I finally had the chance to dig deeper and learn much more about these wonderful cars. The more I read, the more I learned (and continue to learn), and the more I am impressed. What began as my next writing project evolved into a labor of love.

Through this project, I met many others who love their Mercedes-Benz. Some collect them, while others repair or restore the cars. This book represents the collective knowledge that I gained by getting to know these enthusiasts. To my friends in the Mercedes-Benz world, thank you. It really has been a labor of love.

Fred Larimer
Orange, California

Acknowledgments

As with all successful efforts, a strong supporting group is vital. I extend my thanks to a great group of individuals who took time out of their busy days to answer my questions and generously give their help and support. I am grateful for these folks. My thanks go out to every one of you.

My thanks to the staff and management of Caliber Motors (5395 East La Palma Avenue, Anaheim Hills, CA 92807; www.calibermotors.com), and to the following folks for their help and support during this project: Shelly Lazoff, who as it turns out I had known for many years, for arranging cars from the inventory at Caliber Motors for me to photograph; and Ken Brand and Tom Hanson, Caliber Motors, for their help in researching information on the Mercedes-Benz cars featured in this buyer's guide.

Additional thanks to the independent shops that took time from their business needs to answer my questions and teach me more about Mercedes-Benz automobiles: Mesa Performance and Spence, Jim, and Stan Stansfield; Anaheim Hills Autocare and Jim Saunders; Bruce Strauss of Bruce Strauss Auto Care Inc., and his excellent team of mechanics; Silver Star Mercedes Service and Franz Stapley; Marx Service and Steve Marx; and German Auto Repair and Mike Emami.

To the following Mercedes-Benz owners who graciously offered their cars and their time enthusiastically, I thank each of you: Janice and Michael André, Nikola Babovic, Carmeleene and Greg Baguio, Ken Bland, Steve Chapman, Matthew Claus, Marcie and Jack Clinkenbeard, Hugh Curnutt, Philippe de Lespinay, Tez and Doug Dunn, Allan Eggleston and Roger Ross, Mike Emami, Thomas and Binru Fuquay, Kathy and Ralph Gharda, Eva and Scott Gordon, Shahla and Gary Grasso, Craig Goss, George Hansen, Betsy and Dick Hanecak, Barbara and Bob Jackson, Dennis Keith, Diane and Jerry Klayman, Dr. Ron Levin, Patricia and Pat Matthews, Shawn and Chris Macha, Joe Moon, Mark Pyeatte, John S. Piekarczyk, Abbas Salahi, Maria del Carman and Mario Sanchez, Matthew Stockwell, Bruce Strauss, Darlene and Jeff Winegar, and Don York.

To my friends at the Mercedes-Benz Club of America: Judy Abrams, Joe Edone, Rich Schoenfield, and Bob Scudder.

To the friendly and helpful members of the Gullwing group, thank you so very much for helping me locate those sensual W198s.

Thanks go to Fletcher Benton and the good folks at SSF Imported Auto Parts for their help and assistance in chasing down parts prices.

A special thanks to my editors, Peter Bodensteiner and Amy Glaser.

To my friends and relatives: Kathleen and Joe Shematek; Kevin Hite and Klaus Kindor from Crevier BMW in Santa Ana, California; David Boen; Jo Carle; and David Newhardt, for his time, patience, and tips.

To my mentor, Randy Leffingwell, thank you for granting me permission to use the How to Buy section developed for his *Porsche 911 Buyer's Guide* and for his constant and never-ending help with questions, comparing notes, and helping me evolve my skills with photographing cars.

Another big thank you goes to Pamela Welty, the lady in my life who encourages me and keeps me on track.

Introduction

The history of Daimler-Benz (which was later known as DaimlerChrysler after the merger with Chrysler) is well documented. Carl Benz first rode around his workshop grounds in a single-cylinder three-wheeled carriage in 1885, and in early 1886 he received a patent on his Patent-Motorwagen. Gottlieb Daimler's Daimler Motoren Gessellschaft was formed in late 1890, and Benz and Daimler were among the pioneering forces in the emerging automotive industry. When the two companies merged in 1926, they formed the largest automobile manufacturing company in Germany.

The range of cars covered in this buyer's guide focuses on the coupes, convertibles, and SL roadsters from the late 1960s to the 2003 model year.

The early cars covered by this work are fairly straightforward mechanically and electronically. Often repairs can be done with basic tools, a reasonable amount of mechanical ability, and a good workshop manual.

As the cars from the late 1980s and on became more complex and electronically sophisticated, they have become more difficult to repair. As these newer-model cars age and the electronic modules start to break down or fail, the original owner may find that it is actually more financially prudent to trade in a car on a newer model rather than repair a car.

To the second, third, or fourth owners of the vehicle, the high cost of repairing or replacing electronic components will likely be a shock. What this eventually leads to is someone, it is hoped not you, footing the bill to correct improper repairs and make right those repairs that may have been done too cheaply.

In short, the money the buyer may have saved by "bottom-feeding" could very well cost more in the end than if the buyer had paid a bit more for a car in better mechanical shape.

I don't mean to say that you should not buy a late-model Mercedes-Benz. Rather, you should take some time to get to know the cars. Know their good points, weak points, and idiosyncrasies. Learn what to look for, how to spot the good ones, and those that are better left to someone else. Get to know the local Mercedes specialists and mechanics. These folks will save you a lot of grief and money. Buying the Mercedes-Benz of your dreams should be a good experience, and not a nightmare. Read, learn, and become a knowledgeable buyer. It is, after all, your money.

Buying a Used Mercedes

In recent years, the Mercedes-Benz reputation for workmanship and quality has been the subject of much discussion. A number of quality-related problems have surfaced. While some may accept these types of issues in cars from smaller and less established manufacturers, it is not the sort of thing one would expect from Mercedes.

Buyers of pre-owned Mercedes, or any used car, need to keep in mind that a used car is a used car. Some will have been cared for better than others, and there is a story behind every car that is being sold. One thing to keep in mind is that if the deal seems too good to be true, then it probably is.

Information that surfaced during the research for this project revealed several instances of cars that, for one reason or another, were bought back or exchanged by the manufacturer. While these occurrences are rare, it does happen to all manufacturers.

Depending on the circumstances that led to a vehicle being returned to the manufacturer, several fates may await the car. Some may be brought in-house and utilized as development "mules" to test new equipment. Others may be salvaged and sold to businesses that dismantle cars for their parts. Still others may be repaired and made available on the wholesale market. In today's world, cars with this type of a history, when sold by reputable dealers, must have this information disclosed to the public. However, there is no guarantee that by the time the car has made its way through multiple owners this information will be made available to the next individual.

It is in your best interests to have any car you are considering checked by a knowledgeable mechanic and exercise due diligence to validate a car's history before making a decision to buy or not buy.

Model Designations

Mercedes-Benz model designations are confusing to many. Mercedes uses one set of numbers to designate the chassis type and another set of numbers to designate the engine type. These numbers do not directly correlate to the model designations attached to the rear deck lid that many of us are familiar with and use to refer to a particular car (for example, 450SL).

Throughout this buyer's guide you will see many references to the chassis type. In the appendix, a table is provided that will help you become familiar with these various designations. Often, when an owner is ordering parts for his or her car, the person behind the counter will ask what the chassis or engine type is. Mercedes-Benz tends to use the same engines in a variety of cars. An example of this is the engine in the 1995 R129.063 chassis SL320. It is basically the same engine used in the 1995 W124.052 E320 coupe, but some of the ancillaries may not be the same, and some items, like the oil filter or air cleaner or power steering pump, may not be the same. The individual behind the parts counter will need to know this information so the correct part can be ordered. Become familiar with the chassis and engine type(s) of whichever Mercedes-Benz you have. It may save you, and the person behind the parts counter, time and money.

1994 Model Designation Changes

In 1994, Mercedes renamed its entire model lineup. The sequence of the (numeric) model number and (alphabetic) model name were reversed. What was the 500SL in 1993, became the SL500 for 1994. The chassis and engine type designations, with some exceptions, did not change. It was still an R129.067 chassis type, and the engine remained the 119.972 V-8. The model class designations were also updated in 1994 to a more logical and simpler set that remains in place today. The C-class was compact, E-class was executive, and the S-class was super. The SL-class remained the Sport Leicht (light) because it was too familiar to mess with.

On the rear deck lid of most cars you will see the model designation followed by three numbers that denote the engine size in liters. The 2003 C320 Sport Coupe is a good example. It is based on the C-class compact platform and has a 3.2-liter (in this case V-6) engine.

Other examples are the models CLK320 and CLK500. Both are based on the C-class platform, but one has the 3.2-liter V-6 and the other has the 5.0-liter V-8.

Parts Prices

Within each chapter is a list of common parts prices for the specific model(s) covered. Parts prices are quoted for new, factory parts at a suggested list price gathered during research for this project, unless otherwise noted. Mercedes-Benz dealerships are independent franchises, so they are free to set their own pricing structures for parts, which means the prices will vary from one dealer to another. The prices listed are for the parts only and do not include labor to install the parts.

Over time, the prices for the parts listed will change. Remember to use the parts prices as a guide and expect them to change.

Independent repair shops may source their parts from other suppliers, and their prices will likely be different from official Mercedes-Benz prices. Some prices may be lower and some may be higher.

Nonfactory (aftermarket) replacement parts are available for many of the items listed, and often at a reduced price. However, the quality of these parts can vary greatly so be aware of this when considering the use of nonfactory parts.

Buying a Used Mercedes-Benz

The only way to be certain you're buying a solid car is to take it to an authorized dealer or qualified independent service facility for a prepurchase inspection. Make an appointment and expect to pay between $85 and $120 for this examination. A Mercedes-Benz dealer service technician will provide you with a printed list of problems and estimated repair charges for anything they find. You can take this list back to the seller and use it to adjust the selling price. There are things you can check yourself to eliminate flawed candidates. Throughout this section you will be advised to thank the seller for his or her time and walk away. These are cars with problems serious enough to cost you real money to repair. Unless you are an experienced mechanic and are able to do the work yourself, you are probably better served to move on to the next vehicle.

For this screening process, you'll need no tools other than your eyes, ears, and nose. You may want a thermometer for A/C and heating temperature tests to stick into the air vent. A tire gauge will be beneficial too. You might want to bring a flashlight to shine into the engine compartment and a small mirror to hold in places where you cannot get your eyes. Bring along an observant friend to serve as a second pair of eyes and to occupy the seller while you examine their car. Don't be open with the seller. Your color preference or your budget should remain your secret. Don't buy a car at night, because what you can't see, you'll pay for later.

These tests will eliminate dangerous and costly problems. As the car passes each stage, you'll eliminate risks of what may be wrong and you'll understand what is right with the car. You can be more sure you're getting a better car.

A bit of advice here: Don't drive only one of the models you want. Drive at least three, especially if one is beyond your budget. You must build a log of experiences that you have to draw on for that moment when you find the right one at your price.

Begin your inspection with the car body. Rust plagued these cars until the mid-1980s. During your walk-around, look for signs of rust in the lower corners of the wheelwells

and doors. Run your fingers along body seams, door panels, doorjambs, and around the roof. There should be no uneven surfaces, gaps, or seams. Check for gaps and undulations where fixed window (and windshield) seals attach to the body. This could mean the car has had a big accident. Look for paint that appears bubbled below the surface. This indicates rust.

View the entire car from all angles in open shade. Direct sun conceals more than it reveals. Although this may sound a bit cosmic, let the car "talk" to your eyes. The general condition of the exterior, interior, trunk, and engine can tell you volumes about the car if you allow your eyes to "see" the car. If you are viewing the car at the seller's residence, look in the area where the car is kept for oil spots and other visual clues that indicate a conscientious or careless seller. If you are meeting the seller somewhere, try to be there early so you can observe the car as it is driven. Does the car track straight? Is there a cloud of smoke following it? Again, you are looking for clues that would cause you to disqualify a car for possible purchase.

Look at repair records for the life of the car. Be wary if a private owner has no receipts. (Some owners drive their Mercedes for partial business use and need to keep their receipts; you don't need to have them, just look them over.) Used car lots seldom have the records. Authorized dealers can check their computers for service histories, but these will not always reveal history of cosmetic damage.

As you are reviewing past maintenance records, make a note of the names and locations of the shops where work was performed, if possible. Mechanics who were contacted for this book commented on how often they see subpar work. This may be a result of owners taking their cars to the corner service station for repairs, and the individuals performing the work are neither trained to work on the cars nor do they have the proper equipment or tools to properly fix problems.

Everyone consulted for this book agreed that wherever possible and within reason, you should not buy a car that has been crashed. Newer Mercedes-Benz's are unitized construction, meaning that they have no frame. The floorpan, other structural members, and many body panels constitute the frame. The worst case is a car that the insurance company declared a total loss and was salvaged and rebuilt by a body shop. Theft recovery is another kind of salvage. Typically enough of the car has been removed that the insurance company determines it is more cost-effective to replace the car. These cars generally have not been damaged, but are stripped of parts. It will cost you the price of the car plus the parts. If you are a competent mechanic, this may be a good bet; otherwise you'll pay someone a great deal to reinstall what was stolen.

Beginning in 1987 and until just recently, the National Highway Traffic Safety Administration (NHSTA) required that the VIN be marked on specified parts of cars when they were produced. In taking photos of the cars used in this book, whenever possible I have attempted to show the locations of the VIN stickers on the body panels. Learn where to look for these VIN stickers because they will tell you useful information about the car.

Generally speaking, leased vehicles are adequately maintained. Lessors, knowing the car isn't theirs, often drive hard and arrive late for required service intervals. Service records for cars maintained by authorized Mercedes-Benz dealers have been computerized since the 1990s and are retrievable in many cases. However, be cautious as lessors often have no long-term interest in the car and have no motivation to spend money on services for a car they will be giving back in a couple of years. Inspect the car's service manual to see that all warranty period service intervals were met and performed by authorized service facilities. If there are no entries at all in the factory-provided service book, thank the seller for his or her time and leave.

When you inspect the engine, shine your flashlight onto every engine surface you can see. A small mirror will show you the back and undersides. Look for gross evidence of leaks, big smears of oil, or obvious trails of gasoline. Some slight seepage is acceptable. If the rest of the car checks out through this screening process, the prepurchase inspection will catch any leakages and tell you what they signify.

With the engine compartment open, have the seller start the engine. Watch the engine and exhaust pipes (a friend can help you). Does it rock back and forth as the starter engages, suggesting motor mounts have failed? Does it take long to start? Is what comes out of the exhaust pipe(s) white, gray, black, or invisible? On cool or cold mornings, some pale gray steam is normal. As the engine warms, this should stop. A slight puff of white smoke is entirely acceptable. A steady cloud suggests the engine burns oil. Smell the exhaust. If it smells like oil, it is time to thank the owner and leave. Black smoke may come from a vacuum leak, emission system failures, or fuel-injection system malfunctions. All are costly to track down and repair. Black smoke also may indicate an engine loaded up with carbon.

On the later-model cars equipped with on board diagnostics (OBD) systems you will want to perform the following test before starting the engine.

Turn the ignition to the on position and look at the diagnostics displays in the dashboard. The CHECK light(s) should come on and indicate a functioning OBD system. If the CHECK light(s) do not come on, did the owner disable the lights? It has been known to happen. It is ok to perform this test more than once to confirm your observations.

Look for the amber ABS light. It should illuminate and then go out. If it does not light up, it could be a burnt-out bulb or a previous owner may have removed the bulb to mask a nonfunctioning system. If the ABS light remains lit after starting the engine, it indicates an ABS system malfunction that will need to be checked out by a mechanic. It could be as simple as a blown ABS relay internal fuse or something far more serious.

Do not touch the gas pedal when starting a fuel-injected car. If the seller must pump the gas pedal on a fuel-injected engine, this indicates a massive vacuum/air leak that prevents the engine from getting enough fuel to start on its own. This is an expensive problem, and the engine will not pass smog tests in most states. It may burn exhaust valves and perhaps pistons. Shut off the engine (if it even starts) and thank the seller and leave.

Listen for any noise besides a nice exhaust sound, such as tapping, thumping, whirring, or hissing. Let the engine run for 10 minutes and check temperatures. The needle should remain below the halfway point.

Smell for oil, coolant, or gas. If you find any of these, shut the engine off immediately. Some models develop engine compartment gas line leaks that can start a fire. If you didn't smell these critical fluids while the engine was running, turn it off, sniff again, and listen. Crackling sounds coming from the engine suggest the engine is overheating. Water jackets may be clogged, oil may not be circulating properly, the oil cooler may be clogged, or the pump may be failing.

Gurgling sounds suggest problems in the cooling system, such as insufficient flow through the radiator or a failing water pump. The oil cooler or radiator may need cleaning or a replacement. The oil or water pump may need to be replaced.

Check the hoses when the engine is warm and turned off. Don't squeeze the hoses with your fingers because the hoses are hot. Use the eraser end of a pencil or the flat end of a pen to press the hoses. If the hoses are firm when they're hot, they are fine. If the hose is too soft, the inner lining has broken down and the hose will fail sometime soon. If the hose is swollen around the clamps or fittings, this also indicates hose failure.

Next on the list of inspection are the tires, wheels, brake rotors, and suspension. Before you move the car, check the air pressure in all four tires. This will give you the "cold" pressure and it should be within the ranges you'll find on the door-jamb sticker. This also will give you an indication of the seller's attention to routine maintenance. A slight difference is reasonable, but differences of more than 5 or 8 psi from one tire to the next hints at casual care and is not desirable in a previously owned Mercedes-Benz. If tire pressures are off or low, make a note of cold pressures and adjust pressures accordingly at a station before going on the driving test. (More on this in the driving section.) This is necessary to determine if handling ills are tire pressure related or represent much more serious problems.

Rub your hand along the tread on all four tires to feel for ridges or undulations. The ridges will feel like a series of small, short, choppy ski-jumps, and undulations will feel like gently rolling hills and valleys on the tread of the tire. They can occur only in patches or can ring the entire tread. If the surface feels uneven in any way, a closer look on your hands and knees is wise.

Generally someone about to sell their car won't spend $500 to $1,000 to replace tires, so these will tell you a great deal. Be sure they have equal tread depth, are the same brand, and are the appropriate size for the car. Mismatched tires suggest the seller dealt cheaply with other service needs. On the other hand, if the seller has just replaced the tires, this may also be cause for concern. Is the seller trying to hide something?

Ridges on treads indicate poor shock absorber condition. Undulations suggest the alignment is wrong or the suspension is damaged, like from hitting a curb.

On cars with disc brakes, run your finger along the surface of the rotors. You should feel no ridges, just smooth, even surfaces. Feel the outside edge of the rotors. If there is a lip, it suggests the owner has ignored all service warnings that the pads have gone too far and have begun to score the rotors. Depending on the depth of the lip, the rotors may be beyond tolerance. Note this and remember to budget for rotor and pad replacement at your earliest convenience.

If there was no lip, reach inside the wheel wells to feel the inside edge of the wheels. Some alloy wheels will shatter upon impact with a curb. Others distort and can never be trued. If you feel scuffs, bumps, ripples, or cuts on the inside, you may have a bad wheel. Later on, you will be able to better determine what this problem may be during an early portion of the road test.

Next, go to the front of the car. Give a quick, sharp push down on the front bumper. Did you feel any binding or hear any noise except a gentle hiss? As the suspension brings the car back up, does the car clunk or gurgle, or bounce more than once? Does the car rock? It should do none of these. Repeat this on all four corners of the car to make sure that each comes back up at the same rate. If the suspension does not perform smoothly and quietly, make a note to have the mechanic check this and find out what repairs would cost. If the car has passed these tests, you can go on and look inside the passenger compartment.

In the interior, evidence of care or abuse will be more subtle. As you swing open the driver-side door, feel the door in your hand. Does it bind, squeak, or fall as you move it? It should be even, level, and fluid. Check the doorstop where it is bolted to the leading edge of the door. Mercedes-Benz doors have been known to crack where the doorstop attaches (especially on the coupes, because their doors are longer and heavier than sedan doors).

Look at the driver seat around the side edge of the seat cushion or side bolster. If it's cracked or worn, the stitching is broken, or the inner padding is misshapen or lumpy, the car saw mostly short trips around town with frequent driver ingress-egress. Because of this kind of use, the engine rarely reached operating temperature or remained there long enough for the oil to do its true cleaning functions of carrying deposits and debris to the filter. Short hops actually force these deposits onto engine surfaces and bond them into the varnishlike sludge.

Are the door seals cracked, chipped, or split? When rain drips through these onto the carpet, the carpet soaks it up. The top layer of the carpet dries, but the lower layer holds moisture and rusts out the floorboards. This is especially important for the cars from the 1960s and 1970s. If possible, lift the carpets and mats and look for rust. Crawl underneath and look again. Use your mirror to see where you cannot fit.

Now climb into the car. Just sit. Do not touch anything. Close your eyes. Move your body around in the seat and feel if the seat moves, wiggles, or makes noise. If so, the floorpan may have been weakened over time due to a crash or because of rust, which allows play in the seat bolts that should never exist. You should also check the integrity of the seatbelts. They are an element of the handling and cornering security you feel.

Another possibility is that the previous owner was an extremely heavy individual who enjoyed vigorous driving that has stressed the seat frame and mounting bolts. If the seat does wiggle, it is time to thank the owner and leave. Replacing a floorpan is an expense you undertake only if you're completely restoring a car worth the expense.

Now look at the general condition of the interior. Is the leather cracked or dried out? Are knobs and switches cracked or missing? Is any wooden trim cracked and peeling? Hold the steering wheel. Try to pull it from side to side and up and down. There should be no play or movement. Many drivers use steering wheels as handles as they get in or out, which can loosen the steering column mounts.

Adjust the seat to fit your comfort and safety level. In a manual transmission car, make certain you can push the clutch pedal to the floor. (You're not driving yet, but you need the leverage.) Put on the seatbelt and check it for wear, tear, grease, or any slack and play when it is supposed to be holding tight. Fasten and release it a few times to make sure the clasps will not hang up when you need to get out of it. Then, start the car yourself without touching the steering wheel.

The next step is to test the brake pedal and brake system. Do this next section with the engine running. You need engine vacuum boost for the power brake system.

With your hands in your lap, tap on the brake pedal a couple of times to bring the fluid up to pressure. Then press as hard and as far down on the pedal as you can 10 times. Use both legs if you need to. Pedal pressure must remain constant. If the pedal pumps up and gets harder as you pump it, shut off the engine. A rising brake pedal indicates system problems that may include vacuum leaks, water in the brake fluid, a failed brake booster, or a failed hydraulic brake accumulator. If the brakes pass this test, keep pumping as hard as possible. What you are doing now is checking for any movement on the dashboard and listening for creaks and moans.

If there is any noise or movement around the floorboards or in the dash, turn it off, thank the seller, and go home. Crash integrity may have been compromised, possibly through a bad crash or rust damage in the floorboards or firewall.

With the engine running, cycle the automatic transmission through the range of gears. Wait at each selection for a full minute. You should see an rpm drop on the tachometer and feel a slight nudge as gears engage. If it takes 30 seconds for the transmission to catch up to your selection, thank the seller and go home. Do you notice any excessive vibrations from the engine or transmission with the car in gear at idle? This could indicate failed engine mounts or a failed transmission mount.

If the automatic passes the transmission test, hold your foot on the brake and place the gear selector in second gear with the engine at idle. Pull up on the hand brake/parking brake/emergency brake. It should take no more than six to eight clicks with increasing pressure to fully engage the brake. Slowly release pressure on the foot brake pedal and be certain the car does not move. If the car moves or if it requires more than six to eight clicks, make a note to have a mechanic check this during a prepurchase inspection.

You can do this same test for a manual transmission model by easing in the clutch in first or reverse gears. Look around carefully before you try this test to make sure you have plenty of open space if the brake fails. If it takes 15 clicks to engage the brake or the car moves, the rear brake system is worn out and you may need to replace the parking brake shoes or the emergency brake cable.

If everything passes to this point, then, with the engine still at idle, put the car in neutral with the parking brake on. When the temperature gauge moves off the bottom stop (this is important, don't rev the engine when it is cold), give the gas pedal a couple of good raps. Testing this before the engine has reached temperature can mask a sticking throttle cable, which you will find out only when the engine temperature begins to rise. The cables frequently stick if the engine has been steam cleaned. The steam cleaner dissolves all the grease and oil on the engine, good and bad. It usually, however, leaves a residue in the ball-and-cap at the end of the throttle cable at the carburetor linkage or fuel-injection throttle body. This residue can cause a throttle cable to stick.

Now it's time to go on the road test. NOTE: Wearing seatbelts is the law. Insist that anyone who may ride with you on any portion of this test use both seat and shoulder belts. Your first stop on the road test should be a service station if any of the tires were low on air pressure. During the drive to the station, the tires will have heated up slightly. Measure the tire pressure in the low tire again and note the difference between cold pressure and what it is now. The difference will affect how much air you add. For example, if the low tire read 25 psi while cold, but has increased to 27 psi during the drive, that 2 psi difference will affect how much air you add in this way: If the tire specifications call for 32 psi cold, you should inflate this tire to 34 psi for the remainder of your driving test. Do not, however, overinflate the tire beyond what the manufacturer recommends. The maximum psi is engraved into the tire and can be read along the wheel rim.

While that makes common sense, it bears a reminder. In very hot climates, such as Arizona or southern California during the summer, a very low-pressure tire may become very hot if the drive to a service station is some distance at medium or high speed. For example, the 25-psi cold pressure may heat up and rise to 32 or 33 by the time you reach the air pump. Adding those 7 or 8 psi to the 32-psi recommendation may give you 40 psi, a figure that may exceed the manufacturers' maximum recommendation. In that case, go no higher than the maximum and adjust all other tires to match this pressure. You are now ready for the remainder of the road test.

Never road test a car in heavy traffic. You cannot possibly get an accurate impression of the vehicle if you are paying close attention to what other drivers are doing. During the drive, ask the seller (and whomever else may be riding along) to remain quiet. You need to be able to hear the car.

First drive to a smooth stretch of road with a lot of room. Weekends in industrial complexes are best for testing your brakes. These are not panic stops, just routine braking. At 30 miles per hour, brake with a steady even pressure. Check for any undulation in the steering wheel; shaking, pulling from side to side, pulsing or vibrating through the pedal, the noise of metal-on-metal from failed pads, or a chirping sound that indicates cracked brake rotors.

Also check for warped front brake rotors. This is fairly common in some cars, and you may notice this as a shimmy in the steering wheel while braking. It can range from a mild shimmy to a violent shaking during breaking. In most cases, replacing the front rotors and pads will eliminate the shimmy. A side effect of the shimmy if it has not been tended to is that it causes additional stress on the front suspension and can cause premature wear and failure of the shocks and bushings.

Find a potholed road or broken road surface. Listen with your ears and feel with your fingers on the steering wheel as well as the seat of your pants for clunks, rattles, shakes, shimmies, or any unsettling response to potholes or bumps. If doors, side windows, or the back window rattles, it may be tired weather seals or it could be a badly repaired body after a crash. If the car sounds like it's falling apart, it's time to walk away.

In a large empty parking lot, drive in large circles. With your hands at 10 and 2, turn the steering wheel so one hand or the other (you'll do both directions) is at 12. Drive safely, but go fast enough to listen for slight tire squeal. Steering should feel smooth with no chatter in the steering wheel. If it tends to move in the direction of your turn, this is called "falling" and can indicate bent struts.

To find out if you have a bent front wheel, if the car shakes or shimmies when you turn in one direction, the wheel that is bent will be the one outside of the turn. Confirm this by turning in the opposite direction. This unloads the possibly bent wheel and the car should track and ride smoothly. Reconfirm this by resuming the original turn direction. If the car again begins shaking, you have a bent wheel on the outside. Bent wheels most often are on the curb side and inside the wheel. Mercedes-Benz wheels are expensive. Negotiate this in your purchase price.

Listen for and check for any problems with a wheel bearing. If you hear a howling noise while circling in one direction and do not hear it going the other direction, you may be experiencing a bad wheel bearing.

If the car is a mid-1980s or newer car, your dealer or independent shop will check on-board computer systems and determine if the anti-lock braking system (ABS) is functioning properly. If you've never stopped with ABS before, the slowing sensation you will feel is like you've driven into glue. You will feel the brake pedal push back and vibrate against your foot as you hear a rapid, noisy clicking under the dash. The pedal pressure feedback can be unsettling. The clicking is the unit cycling the brakes on and off faster than you can. You may hear rapid tire chirps as the tires near lock-up and then release.

During your braking test, if the car has done anything other than stop in a straight line in a very quick manner, make note of this and have your mechanic check the brake system. If the car does stop quickly with no muss or fuss, continue on to the next phase.

Now, find a quiet alley with walls on both sides to give you the auditory feedback you want here. Drive only at idle speed with both windows open to listen for any noise other than exhaust and tires. If you hear clunking, whirring, tinking, knocking, squeaking, or any other noise besides exhaust purr and tires rolling, walk away.

If the car passes all of these tests, go to a freeway. This is not a high-speed test, but a freeway on-ramp merge test. You want a long freeway entrance ramp where you have great distant vision. You are not seeking record acceleration times, only impressions. The acceleration must be impressive and smooth. There should be no bucking or surging. If the car you drive is not fast and if you do not get a favorable impression of its performance, you are probably better served to thank the seller and move on to the next car.

Exhaust emissions are bigger problems in some states than in others. Check specific requirements in your state before purchasing any automobile. In California, a successful smog test is a condition of purchase; the completed certificate accompanies transfer of title. The seller pays for this test in California. In New York, the vehicle inspection is all-powerful. Whatever your state's standard is, your car must meet it or you cannot get it financed, insured, or licensed.

So, you made it? The car went forward, arrow true, and it stopped on a dime. It made only the noises it was meant to. Well, you've probably found a good one, but you're not done. Return to the seller's driveway because now is the time for the really important stuff.

The Benefits of Living In a Civilized World

Perform this last set of evaluations with the engine idling, the transmission in neutral, and the hand brake on.

Check out both the AM and FM radio frequencies. Bring a cassette and CD with you. Make sure everything works and that it will eject your cassette or CD without drama. If the car has a power antenna, make sure it raises and lowers at least three times without jerking or making loud whirring noises. Older systems and some well-used new ones fail to eject tapes or CDs, and the antennas might not reach maximum extension or retraction after a second run.

Turn on the air conditioning to maximum cold and wait. If leaves or debris blow out the vents, the drip tray near the windshield is cracked and allows water to accumulate in the drip tray and back up into the vents. Routine factory service calls for cleaning these drip trays, but is often missed.

Turn the fan through all speed ranges and wait long enough to make sure they work. Turn the vent back to maximum and insert your turkey thermometer into the air vent. It should read between 32 and 38 degrees. If not, the system, at the least, needs an evacuation, oiling, and recharging. When you take it in for this work, insist the shop do both the evacuation and oiling. A shortcut here can cost you as much as $1,100 later.

To reduce engine temperature, and for your next test, switch off the air and turn the heat and defrost through all speeds to maximum fan speed and maximum heat. Do this even on a 110-degree day or you may discover you have a failed heater core, temperature regulator, or heater/defroster fan on a cold night. These repairs are costly, both for parts and labor.

As you begin to bake, watch the temperature gauge. It should drop slightly. Be alert for radiator coolant or other baking smells inside the car. This could signify a heater core failure or other problems. To make this slightly less challenging for your physical comfort, but even more of a test for the car's electrical system, you can do this portion while checking other important things. Open and close the sunroof at least two times. Do this while the heater/defroster fan is on high. Also, switch the rear window defogger on at this point. The sunroof motor develops a high electric current draw, as does the heater fan. This will let in some cool air as you test the electrical system and fuses while loading the alternator. It should not blow a fuse. If it does, say thanks and goodbye.

If the sunroof motor whines (it will sound like a reeeha-reeeha-reeeha noise), this means the nylon rails or nylon worm drive wheels are failing. Check the weatherstrip around the open roof for tears or car wax buildup. Either of these will allow moisture in. If the roof fails to open or close, it may be anything from a fuse, to a motor, to the switch or wiring, and may be a very reasonable expense or an unreasonable search.

While you're watching the sunroof, look for headliner tears, warped sun visors, stains, or other discoloration on the liner or visors. This indicates moisture already has gotten in. If the sunroof fails to operate or stops while you're testing it, you know what to do.

If the car is a convertible, open and close the top, and make sure the latches work correctly, and that the various motors, hydraulic cylinders, and limit-switches all function properly. Look at the condition of the top, inside and out, for tears, staining, and mildew. Canvas tops are expensive and the labor to install them is not cheap, either. The folding hardtops on the later SL and SLK models are complicated, and adjusting them is not a task for the inexperienced.

Electronics

Some owners have installed aftermarket theft alarms, stereo systems, cellular telephones, radar detectors, and other add-ons. Improperly installed extras can rapidly run down batteries. Cutting into wires, unless you know exactly what you are doing, is a recipe for disaster. Ask the seller if he or she knows who did the work. If it was not a Mercedes dealer, you may want to consider having your local dealer remove and reinstall these items. This becomes more important with each newer model year. Incorrectly wired accessories will drain batteries in a matter of days.

If everything works perfectly, and secretly, it's the color combination you've wanted all your life? Now it's time to "do the deal."

Pricing is a tough issue. Dealers, resellers, and independent service facilities all agree that you should buy the best car you can afford. Mercedes-Benz resale values remain high. They sell for Blue Book retail. Most of these sources recommend spending perhaps $2,000 less than you can afford because you either will want to or need to put that into the car almost immediately, with tires, wheels, or work you want done. Know what you can spend and have all your financing

in order so you can move quickly if, after the inspection, you have found the right car.

Don't take a seller's word that something will be fixed or that the problem really is nothing at all. If the problem is to be fixed, get that in writing and add in writing that you will conclude the deal only if the "problem is fixed to your satisfaction, pending another complete test drive."

The same people who talk about buying the-best-car-you-can-get-and-paying-somewhat-less-than-you-can-afford also suggest you set aside a monthly "allowance" to cover routine and not-so-routine expenses. If you can save $150 a month, when the annual minor and major service bills arrive for $1,500 to $1,600, you won't feel it.

If this entire section seems like an outline of don'ts, that's because you can figure out the do's. There are two important do's. DO thank the seller for his or her time and go home if the car is not up to the standards. DO be patient because most of the cars out there are good ones.

Non-U.S.-Specification Cars—"Gray Market"

During the late 1970s, 1980s, and early 1990s, a niche market existed to import European-specification cars. Known as gray market cars, these cars were often high-performance versions of cars that were marketed and sold in the United States. In order to import euro-spec cars, license, and insure them, the cars had to be brought into compliance with the applicable U.S. EPA and DOT regulations. In many cases, these meant installing side-impact beams in the doors, modifying the bumpers to meet U.S. requirements, changing the lights and instruments, replacing the windshields, and installing smog equipment to meet the EPA requirements.

In some cases, these modifications were carried out in a professional and complete manner and had minimal negative effect on the cars. In other cases, the modifications were done less professionally and have proved problematic. Registering and insuring these cars can be difficult. If the original compliance paperwork is incomplete, you may never be able to register the car for road use, and there are some insurance companies that will not insure these cars.

If the Mercedes-Benz you are looking at should happen to be a European-specification car, you need to know that parts for these cars are often different from cars built to U.S. specifications. As a result, they are not usually stocked by

Mercedes-Benz dealer parts departments. Parts for these euro-spec cars may need to be special-ordered from Germany. Expect these to be more costly and to take longer to arrive at your or your mechanic's doorstep.

Do not let this dissuade you from purchasing a gray market car; just know that these cars are very special and may be more of a challenge than you are prepared for.

1970 280 SL

2002 C230K

Chapter 1

W113 230SL/ 250SL/280SL: 1963–1971
Basic History

Conceived as a replacement for the 190SL and to help bridge the gap created when production of the 300SL ended, the W113-chassis SL was introduced to the world at the March 1963 Geneva Motor Show. Production was in full swing by May 1963, and American customers began receiving cars in the late spring.

The design came from of the drawing table of Paul Bracq and employed a roof design patented by Daimler-Benz. The roof design was nicknamed "Pagoda" because of the tall side windows and concave center section. This balanced the visual effect and served to divert rainwater away from the side windows. The roof design also was strong enough to support a load of more than 2,000 pounds without bending.

The 230SL was available as a roadster with convertible top, a roadster with optional hardtop, or as a coupe. With the introduction of the 2.5-liter, the W113 coupe was discontinued. One 230SL coupe was rebodied by Pininfarina for a German businessman and shown at the 1964 Paris and Turin shows.

Using a pressed-steel floorpan/chassis and a stressed-steel body, the axles and suspension were taken from the Fintail (W111 chassis) sedans. A detachable subframe supported the engine and transmission and was attached to the chassis at three mounting points. Likewise, the engine and transmission used three additional mounting points to attach to the subframe.

Early cars had the spare tire mounted vertically on the left side. Beginning in October 1964, the spare was relocated to the right side of the trunk floor to make way for a larger fuel tank.

Available with either a four-speed manual or an optional four-speed automatic, many of these SLs were equipped with the automatic. Beginning in January 1966, a five-speed overdrive manual transmission was available as an option. A small number of SLs were ordered with this transmission, and finding one would be a rare surprise. Several rear axle ratios were available, as well as a limited slip.

Front suspension is unequal-length A-arms, coil springs, and gas-shocks. Rear suspension used a low, single-pivot axle, coil springs, gas-shocks, and a compensator spring. Power-assisted steering was available as an option and was a popular addition.

The 230SL was equipped with hydraulic-assisted brakes, with discs in front and drums in the rear. When the 250SL was introduced, discs were at all four corners. The 14-inch wheel size was considered unusual for the times, and tire companies had to be convinced to produce a tire especially for these cars.

Front seating is individual bucket seats with leather seats and door panels. Behind the seats a carpeted parcel tray for smaller items supplements the storage space available in the trunk. A rear bench seat was an option, but it didn't leave room for storing the folding top and was available only in conjunction with the removable hardtop.

The dash includes a tachometer on the left and a speedometer on the right that flank a vertical stack of gauges to monitor temperature, oil pressure, battery, and gas. The centrally mounted radio is below a pair of ventilation slide levers, and an analog clock and glove box are to the right of the radio. Matching circular air outlets are at the outboard ends of the dash, and smaller window vents are also provided.

At the rear of the passenger compartment is the convertible top stowage well that has a finished metal cover to hide the top from view. The removable hardtop has four latching points and requires either a lift or two people to remove and store.

The 230SL engine and transmission were drafted from the 220SE and were slightly overbored (2 millimeters) with larger valves, revised valve timing, and higher compression. The four-main bearing 2,306-cc/140.9-ci SOHC four-cylinder produced 170 brake horsepower at 5,600 revolutions. Departing from the norm, this was the first Mercedes-Benz to use an alternator in place of a generator.

Production of the 230SL ended in January 1967, and the 250SL was in the showrooms not long after. The coupe version was discontinued when the 2.5-liter SL was introduced. The detachable hardtop continued to be available as an option.

The 2.5-liter M129 engine came directly from the S-class sedans. The smooth-running six delivered better acceleration, had an extra 3-mile-per-hour top speed, and featured a seven-bearing crank, longer stroke, increased torque, and improved drivability.

Wheel width was increased to 6 inches for the SL class. The brakes were upgraded to four-wheel discs with a pressure-regulator to help prevent rear brake lock-up. Other running improvements included a revised steering wheel hub and energy-absorbing steering column, three-point seatbelts, new carpeting and door pockets, improved lighting for heater controls, lighted shift quadrant, and removable latch handles for the hard and soft tops on the windshield header. Production of the 250SL ran for one year, and 5,196 cars were produced.

The 280SL began production in early 1968 and ended in March 1971 with 23,885 cars produced. Nearly 13,000 were imported to the United States, which was slightly more than half the production.

Using the same M130 engine as in S-class sedans but with fuel injection in place of the carburetor, 280SL drivers received an additional 10 brake horsepower over the 250SL. North American emissions controls began in 1968 and resulted in a hotter-running 2.8-liter engine. Mercedes-Benz fitted a larger cooling system, and a viscous-coupled, thermostatically controlled fan was added in 1969 to address possible overheating.

The tires were now conventional radials instead of special-sized bias ply tires that were used on the 230 and 250 models. The option list included power-assisted steering, leather seats, mats, bumper guards, stereo radio, tinted glass, and air conditioning. A limited-slip was also available, and a new five-speed overdrive could be ordered after September 1969.

Pagoda SLs didn't have all the amenities of the newer cars, but they still were great cars. Parts are still readily available, so restoring one is certainly an option, and there are many that already have all, if not most, of the work completed. The design has worn well over the years.

This is a properly restored 1967 230SL. The locking gas cap is period-correct. Gaps between panels should be even and consistent. Look for rust anywhere water could get trapped.

When properly restored, the interior should look like this 1967 230SL. The carpeting has been replaced, and the door panels and seats have been recovered in correct materials and in the same colors as when the car was originally delivered in January 1967.

Remember to let the fuel pump run for about 30 seconds to pressurize lines before starting the engine. The overflow tank for the 230SL is the brass canister at the right rear of the engine compartment.

Early cars had a spare tire mounted upright on the left side. Later cars, like this one, have it lying down in the trunk. Lift the mats and look for evidence of rust, which is a sign that the trunk seal leaks. Original tool kits are hard to find. The underside of the trunk lid and the exposed metal in the trunk should all be painted black.

Under the hood, this car shows its age. Look for oil, fuel line, and radiator hose leaks. The firewall cover is original and has cracked from age and engine compartment heat. Examine the throttle linkage for binding and sticking.

The VIN plate for 250SL is riveted on at the forward edge of the left doorjamb. Confirm the car has the correct chassis—113.043 for a 250SL. Check the condition of the door stop and look for any evidence of rust.

Here is a close-up of the dash. Compare this to the photos of the 230SL (page 18) to note wear from sun exposure. The radio is not an original. The metallic studs are for a fitted canvas cover that can be attached when the top is removed.

Shown here is the rear of a 250SL. The gas cap is a replacement. Look for evidence of rust in the lower extremities. The taillight lenses on the 250SL switched to amber turn-signal elements.

This is a European-spec 250SL. Originally delivered to France, the Marchal driving lights have yellow bulbs. Note the front bumper is not straight, which might indicate minor damage or improper repairs. Check the car thoroughly for rust.

This European-spec 250SL features an optional rear bench seat. Cars equipped with this have no soft top because there is no room for the stowage well. Passenger legroom is minimal, so getting in and out is difficult.

Here is an interior detail of this European-specification 250SL. The speedometer is marked in kilometers per hour, and the center cluster gauges have metric markings. The radio has been replaced by an aftermarket unit.

This 1970 280SL has been completely restored. Its classic lines still look good today. Check gaps around the doors, hood, and trunk lid. They should be even and consistent.

This is the rear of a 1970 280SL. Perfect chrome, perfect paint, and a great sunset. This car has been completely restored. Check the gaps around the doors, hood, and trunk lid. They should be even and consistent.

Here is the interior of a 1970 280SL. The factory air conditioning unit mounts under the dash. This is what a correct car should be like. It has the correct radio, OE carpeting, and upholstery. Check the windshield wipers for operation. The repairs are sinfully expensive.

This is a 1970 280SL trunk. Remove the spare and lift the mats to check for any rust. Confirm the presence of a rolled-up tool kit. Replacements are hard to find. Check the condition of shock towers and look for evidence of rust.

Common Parts List
W113 230SL, 1963–1966

Engine:

Oil filter	$4.60
Fuel filter	$11.00
Fuel pump (electric)	$645.00
Starter	$177.00 (rebuilt)
Alternator	$113.00 (rebuilt)
Water pump	
w/viscous clutch	$161.00
w/o fan clutch	$199.00

Exhaust:

Center muffler	$398.00
Rear muffler	$236.00

Chassis:

Brake master	$248.00
Front rotor	$132.00 each
Front pads (set)	
w/ATE caliper	$30.00
w/three-piston caliper	$81.00
Front shocks	$158.00 each
Rear shocks	$158.00 each

Common Parts List
W113 250SL, 1966–1968

Engine:

Oil filter	$4.60
Fuel filter	$11.00
Fuel pump (electric)	$645.00
Starter	$177.00 (rebuilt)
Alternator	$113.50 (rebuilt)
Water pump	$161.00
Fan clutch	$238.00

Exhaust:

Center muffler	$398.00
Rear muffler	$236.00

Chassis:

Brake master	$266.00
Front rotor	$93.00 each
Front pads (set)	$30.00
Front shocks	$158.00 each
Rear shocks	$158.00 each

Technical Specifications
W113 230SL, 1963–1966

Engine:

Type	Inline-six cylinder, SOHC
Displacement cc/ci	2,306/140.9
Compression ratio	9.3:1
Bhp @ rpm	170 @ 5,600
Torque ft-lb @ rpm	159 @ 4,500
Injection type	Bosch
Fuel requirement	Premium

Chassis/drivetrain:

Transmission:	
Automatic	Four-speed automatic
Manual	Four-speed syncromesh
Steering	Recirculating ball, power-assist optional
Front suspension	Independent w/unequal-length A-arms, coil springs, tube shocks, anti-roll bar
Rear suspension	Independent w/single-pivot swing axles, coil springs, tube shocks, compensator spring
Differential:	
Automatic	3.75:1
Manual	3.75:1

General:

Wheelbase	94.5
Weight:	
Automatic	2,905 pounds (est.)
Manual	2,855 pounds (est.)
Wheels	Steel disc, 14x6.5
Tires	185-14
Brake system:	
Front	10.0-inch Girling disc brakes
Rear	9.0 Alfin drums
0–60 mph:	
Automatic	11.0 sec (est.)
Manual	10.1 sec (est.)
Maximum speed mph	115
Fuel tank capacity	17.2 gal

Fuel economy:

EPA estimated mpg:	
Automatic	18.0–22.0 mpg
Manual	16.0–24.0 mpg

Rating Chart
W113 230SL/250SL/ 280SL, 1963–1971

Model	Comfort/Amenities	Reliability	Collectibility	Parts/Service Availability	Est. Annual Repair Costs
230SL	★★★	★★★↓	★★★↓	★★★↓	★★★
250SL	★★★	★★★↓	★★★★	★★★↓	★★★
280SL	★★★	★★★↓	★★★↓	★★★↓	★★★

Common Parts List
W113 280SL, 1968–1971

Engine:

Oil filter	$4.60
Fuel filter	$11.00
Fuel pump (electric)	$645.00
Starter	$177.00 (rebuilt)
Alternator	$113.50 (rebuilt)
Water pump	$161.00
Fan clutch	$238.00

Exhaust:

Center muffler	$398.00
Rear muffler	$236.00

Chassis:

Brake master	$248.00
Front rotor	$93.00 each
Front pads (set)	$30.00
Front shocks	$158.00 each
Rear shocks	$158.00 each

Technical Specifications:
W113 250SL, 1966–1968

Engine:

Type	Inline-six cylinder, SOHC
Displacement cc/ci	2,496/152.3
Compression ratio	9.5:1
Bhp @ rpm	170 @ 5,600
Torque ft-lb @ rpm	174 @ 4,500
Injection type	Bosch
Fuel requirement	Premium

Chassis/drivetrain:

Transmission:	
Automatic	Four-speed automatic
Manual	Four-speed syncromesh
Steering	Recirculating ball, power assist optional
Front suspension	Independent w/unequal-length A-arms, coil springs, tube shocks, anti-roll bar
Rear suspension	Independent w/single-pivot swing axles, coil springs, tube shocks, compensator spring
Differential:	
Automatic	3.92:1
Manual	3.69:1

General:

Wheelbase	94.5
Weight:	
Automatic	3,059 pounds (est.)
Manual	2,998 pounds (est.)
Wheels	Steel disc, 14x6.5
Tires	185-14
Brake system:	
Front	10.7-inch vented disc brakes
Rear	11.0-inch vented disc brakes
0–60 mph:	
Automatic	N/A
Manual	9.5 sec (est.)
Maximum speed mph	115 (est.)
Fuel tank capacity	21.7 gal
Fuel economy:	
EPA estimated mpg:	
Automatic	N/A
Manual	18.0–22.0 mpg

Technical Specifications:
W113 280SL, 1967–1971

Engine:

Type	Inline-six cylinder, SOHC
Displacement cc/ci	2,778/169.5
Compression ratio	9.5:1
Bhp @ rpm	180 @ 5,700
Torque ft-lb @ rpm	193 @ 4,500
Injection type	Bosch mechanical
Fuel requirement	Premium

Chassis/drivetrain:

Transmission:	
Automatic	Four-speed automatic
Manual	Four-speed syncromesh
Optional	ZF five-speed syncromesh
Steering	Recirculating ball, power assist optional
Front suspension	Independent w/unequal-length A-arms, coil springs, tube shocks, anti-roll bar
Rear suspension	Independent w/single-pivot swing axles, coil springs, tube shocks, compensator spring
Differential:	
Automatic	3.92:1
Manual	3.69:1

General:

Wheelbase	94.5
Weight:	
Automatic	3,420 pounds (est.)
Manual	3,120 pounds (est.)
Wheels	Steel disc, 14x6.5
Tires	185-14
Brake system:	
Front	10.7-inch vented disc brakes
Rear	11.0-inch vented disc brakes
0–60 mph:	
Automatic	10.3 sec (est.)
Manual	10.3 sec (est.)
Maximum speed mph	115 (est.)
Fuel tank capacity	21.7 gal

Fuel economy:

EPA estimated mpg:	
Automatic	N/A
Manual	16.0–19.0 mpg

Hardtops—These are prone to rusting. Check the rear B-pillars inside and out for rusting. Water can get trapped in and under the chrome trim and lead to rust. Look on the inside of the top and in the lower rear corners. Is the top liner discolored? It could be a sign of past water leaks or damage. Tops are no longer available and the only way to get one is to buy one secondhand.

Soft top—Look for rust in the storage well for the convertible top. The tonneau locking mechanism is difficult to set up right. Also check the mechanical release mechanism for function and adjustment.

Trunk seals—They deteriorate over time, so check under mats and in corners for any signs of water infiltration or rusting.

Heater controls—Check them for operation because replacement parts are hard to locate.

Windshield wipers—Check them for operation. Repairs require removing the dashboard to gain access, which is labor intensive and expensive to repair.

Electrical switches—Check for proper operation. With underhood electrics, moisture and age can result in worn-out alternators and voltage regulators. Check electrical wiring for fraying, deteriorated insulation, and the like.

Service history—Obtain as much as you can. Find out the mechanic the previous owner(s) used. He or she may have additional history on the car that will help.
Cosmetic note—The painted centers of the hubcaps originally coordinated with the soft top. The top and hubcaps should match with each other.

VIN—Check the metal plate riveted left front fender inner panel. It lists color code and other information. 230SL VIN plate is attached to the cowl in the engine compartment. 280SL VIN plate is in the left doorjamb. Both contain the chassis type and build date.

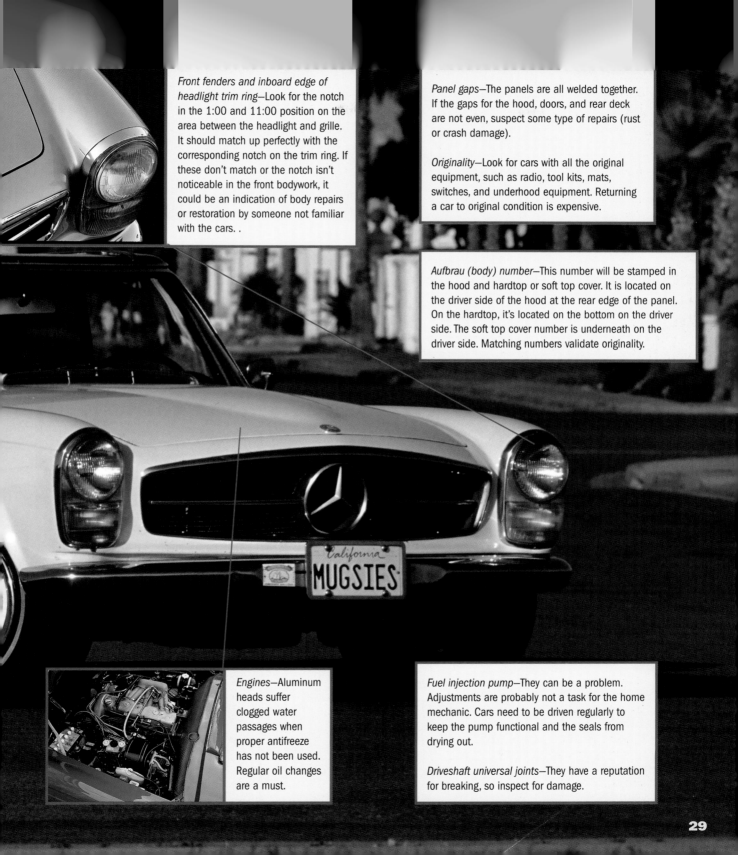

Front fenders and inboard edge of headlight trim ring—Look for the notch in the 1:00 and 11:00 position on the area between the headlight and grille. It should match up perfectly with the corresponding notch on the trim ring. If these don't match or the notch isn't noticeable in the front bodywork, it could be an indication of body repairs or restoration by someone not familiar with the cars. .

Panel gaps—The panels are all welded together. If the gaps for the hood, doors, and rear deck are not even, suspect some type of repairs (rust or crash damage).

Originality—Look for cars with all the original equipment, such as radio, tool kits, mats, switches, and underhood equipment. Returning a car to original condition is expensive.

Aufbrau (body) number—This number will be stamped in the hood and hardtop or soft top cover. It is located on the driver side of the hood at the rear edge of the panel. On the hardtop, it's located on the bottom on the driver side. The soft top cover number is underneath on the driver side. Matching numbers validate originality.

Engines—Aluminum heads suffer clogged water passages when proper antifreeze has not been used. Regular oil changes are a must.

Fuel injection pump—They can be a problem. Adjustments are probably not a task for the home mechanic. Cars need to be driven regularly to keep the pump functional and the seals from drying out.

Driveshaft universal joints—They have a reputation for breaking, so inspect for damage.

Chapter 2

W107 350SL 4.5 450SL/380SL/ 560SL: 1971–1989
Basic History

Introduced in 1971 and nicknamed *der Panzerwagen* by Mercedes engineers, the W107 chassis was a completely new design. The 4.5-liter V-8 engine was new, and a three-speed automatic was the only transmission available for the U.S. market.

The chassis is a unit body design that featured front and rear crush-zones, door mounts that are more resistant to side impact forces, and the fuel tank was moved forward to between the rear wheels. It was a much safer design.

Standard equipment included air conditioning, automatic transmission, power steering, power brakes, and a soft or hardtop with heated rear glass and fog lights. An optional rear seat was available, but it was cramped. About the only way an adult could ride back there was to sit sideways.

The new SL, built on a 2.4-inch-longer wheelbase, is 0.5 inches wider and 0.2 inches lower than the 280SL Pagoda. The extra length and width came with a penalty—weight. Heavier than the 280SL by 300 pounds, the extra weight was a result of a stronger structure and the need to meet U.S. DOT crash-protection standards of the time.

A four-passenger version, the 350SLC 4.5, offered usable rear seating, but was available only as a coupe. Perhaps better thought of as a 2+2, the SLC was developed in tandem with the SL. The SLC's wheelbase is 14.2 inches longer, with the added length between the rear wheels and the doors.

Improved heating and ventilation systems were designed to use the same ducting for heated and conditioned air. This improved HVAC system also channeled heated or cooled air into and through the door panels. Although it was state of the art in the early 1970s, by today's standards, the system is barely adequate on hot summer days.

The windshield pillars, although steeply raked and visually thin, were designed using computer analysis to provide maximum occupant protection in the event of a rollover. The typical Mercedes attention to detail resulted in rain gutters that channel rainwater up and over the roof and help minimize moisture collecting on the side windows.

Ribbed lower body panels prevent water, dirt, and debris from collecting on the sides and rear of the car. The taillights are also designed to be self-cleaning. The U.S.-spec cars received four round headlamps, while European cars received single, flush-mounted headlamps. Many cars have been retrofitted with the European lenses, and while these lights are more effective than standard U.S. lighting, they may not be approved in all areas of the country. Check your local DMV laws regarding use of these lights.

The W107 was renamed as the 450SL and 450SLC for 1973, which more correctly reflected the 4.5-liter V-8. Throughout production the body remained basically the same. The most obvious change was the addition of DOT-mandated 5-mile-per-hour bumpers for the 1974 model year. The early cars were equipped with steel wheels and wheel covers. Optional alloy wheels became standard equipment for 1976, but many of the early cars have since had the alloy wheels installed in place of the original steel rims.

Automatic climate control came onboard in 1978, and while it was more effective than the original system, it is more complex and prone to problems with the electronic servos and vacuum-operated flaps. Check the system for proper operation because diagnosis and repairs can be labor intensive and expensive.

In 1981, the 4.5-liter V-8 was replaced by an aluminum-block 3.8-liter V-8. This smaller-displacement V-8, while more fuel efficient and lighter weight, had single-row chain drives for the overhead camshafts. Unfortunately, these single-row chains are prone to stretching, particularly if the engine oil is not changed regularly, and could lead to the chain jumping a tooth. When this occurs, the usual result is valve-to-piston contact and substantial, serious engine damage. The single-row timing chains were discontinued in 1983, and beginning in 1984, double-row chains were used.

Introduced in 1986, the 560SL received revised front suspension geometry, and in the rear the MBZ torque-compensating axle reduced squat and lift. The rear differential mounting was improved to further quiet the infamous rear-axle "SL-whine."

A limited-slip was now standard, and alloy wheels were now 15x7 inches. A four-speed automatic was standard equipment, as was leather upholstery. Supplemental restraint (air bag), knee bolsters below the dash, and ABS were standard equipment, as was the automatic climate control and an AM/FM stereo cassette. The roughly 46 percent power increase offered by the 5.6-liter V-8 also resulted in a Gas Guzzler Tax of about $1,300 that was incorporated into the sticker price. Visually, an under-bumper chin spoiler improved aerodynamics, and a third brake light was added to the rear deck lid.

Production of the W107 chassis ended in 1989, and more than 230,000 cars were built since its introduction in 1971.

Gray Market Cars

The higher-performance European SLs, in particular the 500SL, were not officially imported to the United States, but many were imported and federalized by private parties. In some cases, the required modifications were made in a complete and professional manner and had minimal negative effect on the cars. In other cases, the work was done less professionally. If the W107 you are looking at is a gray market import, make sure you confirm that all of the appropriate DOT and EPA paperwork is available and complete or else you may never be able to register and insure the vehicle.

The hood emblem and grille leave little doubt that this is a Mercedes Benz. The 450SL was right at home in posh neighborhoods.

The ribbed design of taillights help keep the lens clean. The wraparound design functioned as both turn signal and side marker. The 1971 cars were badged as 350SL 4.5s, and the 1972 cars were rebadged as the 450SL.

There is much to look for in the engine compartment. Check the VIN stamped on the radiator core support, the body and paint tag, the condition of rubber vacuum lines, the brake reservoir for condition of brake fluid, the radiator and its hoses, and the coolant level and color. All are indications of proper care and maintenance.

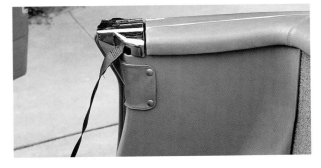

The connector for the hardtop's heated rear window plugs into the electrical receptacle behind the passenger seat. Check for damage, because it is an easy item to forget about when removing the hardtop. The shoulder belt attaching point is underneath the neatly finished trim.

The dash cover protects the top of the dashboard from UV damage. Remove the floor mats to check for moisture. If it is damp, check for rust in the floorboards.

Chromed alloys on this 1984 380SL are a nice touch.

Do not let the dust put you off. The important info is the VIN (lower right corner). Also visible is the body and paint tag (center, in front of the radiator) and an R134a conversion tag (on the radiator shroud).

The 450SLC interior is spacious and well laid out. The ducts that feed air to the doors are visible at 3:00 and 9:00 positions. The early-style HVAC controls are visible in the center of the dash. The armrest shows some wear, but check under sheepskins for the condition of the leather. Look under the floor mats for evidence of trapped moisture and rusted floorboards.

Leather and wood surrounds the occupants. The analog clock is in place of the center vent of earlier cars. The HVAC in this 1984 380SL is the more modern climate control system. Check the system for proper operation, because it is expensive to diagnose and repair.

This sticker on the radiator overflow carries a warning tag that reminds owners to use coolant approved for use with alloy engine blocks and aluminum radiators.

This is the VIN sticker in the driver-side doorjamb. Make sure that the VINs match, and look for the tire pressure sticker. Check around for any signs of overspray, which is a possible clue to accident-related repairs.

This is the engine compartment of the 1988 560SL. Check the radiator plastic tanks for evidence of leakage. The presence of factory emissions stickers confirms this is a U.S. specification model. The VIN should match the sticker in the doorjamb and on the left windshield pillar. The punch-plate carries the color and trim codes.

The steering wheel contains the driver-side airbag. The carpeted knee bolster below the dash is there to protect the driver in the event of an accident. The black plastic rectangle in the doorjamb is the duct to carry conditioned air into the doors.

Technical Specifications: W107 350SL 4.5, 1971–1972

Engine:

Type	SOHC 90-degree V-8
Displacement cc/ci	4,520/275.8
Compression ratio	8.0:1
Bhp @ rpm	195 @ 4,500
Torque ft-lb @ rpm	259 @ 3,000
Injection type	Bosch electronic
Fuel requirement	Regular, 91 octane

Chassis/drivetrain:

Transmission	three-speed automatic
Steering	Recirculating ball, power-assisted
Front suspension	Unequal-length A-arms, coil springs, tube shocks, anti-roll bar
Rear suspension	Semi-trailing arms, coil springs, tube shocks, anti-roll bar
Differential	3.07:1

General:

Wheelbase	96.9
Weight	3,905 pounds
Wheels	Steel disc, 14x6.5
Tires	205/70VR-14
Brake system:	Four-wheel disc, vacuum-assisted
Front	10.8-inch vented discs
Rear	11.0-inch solid discs
0–60 mph:	
Automatic	10.5 sec
Maximum speed mph	124
Fuel capacity, U.S. gallons	23.8

Fuel economy:

EPA estimated mpg	13.2 mpg

Technical Specifications: W107 350SLC 4.5, 1972–1973

Engine:

Type	SOHC 90-degree V-8
Displacement cc/ci	4,520/275.8
Compression ratio	8.0:1
Bhp @ rpm	195 @ 4,500
Torque ft-lb @ rpm	259 @ 3,000
Injection type	Bosch electronic
Fuel requirement	Regular, 91 octane

Chassis/drivetrain:

Transmission	three-speed automatic
Steering	Recirculating ball, power-assisted
Front suspension	Unequal-length A-arms, coil springs, tube shocks, anti-roll bar
Rear suspension	Semi-trailing arms, coil springs, tube shocks, anti-roll bar
Differential	3.07:1

General:

Wheelbase	111.0
Weight	4,085 pounds
Wheels	Steel disc, 14x6.5
Tires	205/70VR-14
Brake system:	Four-wheel disc, vacuum-assisted
Front	10.8-inch vented discs
Rear	11.0-inch solid discs
0–60 mph:	
Automatic	10.5 sec
Maximum speed mph	124
Fuel capacity, U.S. gallons	23.8

Fuel economy:

EPA estimated mpg	15.5 mpg

Common Parts List
350SL 4.5/350SLC 4.5, 1971

Engine:

Oil filter	$8.00
Fuel filter	$45.00
Fuel pump(s):	
w/CIS	$284.00
w/EFI	$625.00
Starter	$209.00 (rebuilt)
Alternator	$308.00
Fan clutch	$460.00
Water pump	$155.50

Body:

Front bumper:	
Bumper end—left	$97.00
Bumper end—right	$97.00
Bumper guard—left	$73.00
Bumper guard—right	$73.00
Bumper molding	$308.00
Hood	$2,060.00
Left front fender	$525.00
Rear bumper:	
Bumper end—left	$122.00
Bumper end—right	$122.00
Bumper guard—left	$42.00
Bumper guard—right	$42.00
Bumper molding	$308.00

Windshield	$1,023.00
Headlight assembly	$540.00
Taillight lens	$244.00

Exhaust:

Center muffler	$442.00
Rear muffler	$456.00

Chassis:

Brake master	$350.00
Front rotor	$112.00 each
Front pads (set)	$48.00
Front shocks	$137.00 each
Rear shocks	$140.00 each

Technical Specifications: W107 450SL, 1972–1980

Engine:

Type	SOHC 90-degree V-8
Displacement cc/ci	4,520/275.8
Compression ratio	8.0:1
Bhp @ rpm	195 @ 4,500
Torque ft-lb @ rpm	259 @ 3,000
Injection type	Bosch electronic
Fuel requirement	Regular, 91 octane

Chassis/drivetrain:

Transmission	three-speed automatic
Steering	Recirculating ball, power-assisted
Front suspension	Unequal-length A-arms, coil springs, tube shocks, anti-roll bar
Rear suspension	Semi-trailing arms, coil springs, tube shocks, anti-roll bar
Differential	3.07:1

General:

Wheelbase	96.9
Weight	3,905 pounds
Wheels	Steel disc, 14x6.5
Tires	205/70VR-14
Brake system:	Four-wheel disc, vacuum-assisted
Front	10.8-inch vented discs
Rear	11.0-inch solid discs
0–60 mph:	
Automatic	10.5 sec
Maximum speed mph	124
Fuel capacity, U.S. gallons	23.8
Fuel economy:	
EPA estimated mpg	12 to 19 mpg

Technical Specifications: W107 450SLC, 1973–1980

Engine:

Type	SOHC 90-degree V-8
Displacement cc/ci	4520/275.8
Compression ratio	8.0:1
Bhp @ rpm	195 @ 4,500
Torque ft-lb @ rpm	259 @ 3,000
Injection type	Bosch electronic
Fuel requirement	Regular, 91 octane

Chassis/drivetrain:

Transmission	three-speed automatic
Steering	Recirculating ball, power-assisted
Front suspension	Unequal-length A-arms, coil springs, tube shocks, anti-roll bar
Rear suspension	Semi-trailing arms, coil springs, tube shocks, anti-roll bar
Differential	3.07:1

General:

Wheelbase	111.0
Weight	4,085 pounds
Wheels	Steel disc, 14x6.5
Tires	205/70VR-14
Brake system:	Four-wheel disc, vacuum-assisted
Front	10.8-inch vented discs
Rear	11.0-inch solid discs
0–60 mph:	
Automatic	10.5 sec
Maximum speed mph	124
Fuel capacity, U.S. gallons	23.8
Fuel economy:	
EPA estimated mpg	12 to 19 mpg

Common Parts List
450SL/450SLC, 1972–1980

Engine:

Oil filter	$8.00
Fuel filter	$45.00
Fuel pump(s):	
w/CIS	$284.00
w/EFI	$625.00
Starter	$209.00 (rebuilt)
Alternator	$308.00
Fan clutch	$460.00
Water pump	$155.50

Body:

Front bumper:	
Bumper end—left	$97.00
Bumper end—right	$97.00
Bumper guard—left	$73.00
Bumper guard—right	$73.00
Bumper molding	$308.00
Hood	$2,060.00
Left front fender	$525.00
Rear bumper:	
Bumper end—left	$122.00
Bumper end—right	$122.00
Bumper guard—left	$42.00
Bumper guard—right	$42.00
Bumper molding	$308.00

Windshield	$1,023.00
Headlight assembly	$540.00
Taillight lens	$244.00

Exhaust:

Catalytic converter	$795.00 (rebuilt)
Front muffler	$442.00
Rear muffler	$456.00

Chassis:

Brake master	$350.00
Front rotor	$112.00 each
Front pads (set)	$48.00
Front shocks	$137.00 each
Rear shocks	$140.00 each

Rating Chart
W107 SLs, 1971–1989

Model	Comfort/Amenities	Reliability	Collectibility	Availability	Est. Annual Repair Costs
350SL	★★★★½	★★★	★★★½	★★★½	★★★½
350SLC	★★★★½	★★★	★★★½	★★★½	★★★½
450SL	★★★½	★★★★	★★★½	★★★½	★★★½
450SLC	★★★½	★★★★	★★★½	★★★½	★★★½
380SL	★★★★	★★★★	★★★	★★★½	★★★½
560SL	★★★★	★★★★	★★★½	★★★½	★★★½

Technical Specifications: W107 380SL, 1981–1985

Engine:

Type	SOHC 90-degree V-8, aluminum block
Displacement cc/ci	3,839/234.3
Compression ratio	8.3:1
Bhp @ rpm	155 @ 4,750
Torque ft-lb @ rpm	196 @ 2,750
Injection type	Bosch K-Jetronic
Fuel requirement	Unleaded, 91 octane

Chassis/drivetrain:

Transmission	Four-speed automatic
Steering	Recirculating ball, power-assisted
Front suspension	Unequal-length A-arms, coil springs, tube shocks, anti-roll bar
Rear suspension	Semi-trailing arms, coil springs, tube shocks, anti-roll bar
Differential	2.47:1

General:

Wheelbase	96.9
Weight	3,555 pounds
Wheels	Cast alloy, 14x6.5J
Tires	205/70HR-14
Brake system:	Four-wheel disc, vacuum-assisted
Front	10.8-inch vented discs
Rear	11.0-inch solid discs
0–60 mph:	
Automatic	10.9 sec
Maximum speed mph	110
Fuel capacity, U.S. gallons	22.5
Fuel economy:	
EPA estimated mpg	16 to 22 mpg

Common Parts List 380SL, 1983–1985

Engine:

Oil filter	$8.00
Fuel filter	$45.00
Fuel pump(s)	$284.00
Starter	$209.00 (rebuilt)
Alternator	$308.00 (rebuilt)
Radiator	$925.00
Fan clutch	$460.00
Water pump	$248.00

Body:

Front bumper:	
Bumper end—left	$97.00
Bumper end—right	$97.00
Bumper guard—left	$73.00
Bumper guard—right	$73.00
Bumper molding	$308.00
Hood	$2,060.00
Left front fender	$525.00
Rear bumper:	
Bumper end—left	$122.00
Bumper end—right	$122.00
Bumper guard—left	$42.00
Bumper guard—right	$42.00
Bumper molding	$308.00
Windshield	$1,023.00
Headlight assembly	$540.00
Taillight lens	$244.00

Exhaust:

Catalytic converter	$425.00 each (rebuilt)
Front muffler	$442.00
Rear muffler	$456.00

Chassis:

Brake master	$278.00
Front rotor	$94.00 each
Front pads (set)	$48.00
Front shocks	$137.00 each
Rear shocks	$140.00 each

Technical Specifications: W107 560SL, 1986–1989

Engine:

Type	SOHC 90-degree V-8, aluminum block
Displacement cc/ci	5,547/338.5
Compression ratio	9.0:1
Bhp @ rpm	227 @ 4,750
Torque ft-lb @ rpm	279 @ 3,250
Injection type	Bosch KE-Jetronic
Fuel requirement	Unleaded, 92 octane

Chassis/drivetrain:

Transmission	Four-speed automatic
Steering	Recirculating ball, power-assisted
Front suspension	Unequal-length A-arms, coil springs, tube shocks, anti-roll bar
Rear suspension	Semi-trailing arms, coil springs, tube shocks, anti-roll bar, torque-compensating axle
Differential	2.47:1

General:

Wheelbase	96.7
Weight	3,880 pounds
Wheels	Cast Alloy, 15x7J
Tires	205/65VR-15
Brake system:	Four-wheel disc, vacuum-assisted w/ABS
Front	10.9-inch vented discs
Rear	11.0-inch solid discs
0–60 mph:	
Automatic	7.5 sec
Maximum speed mph	130 (@ 4,000 rpm)
Fuel capacity, U.S. gallons	22.5
Fuel economy:	
EPA estimated mpg	15 to 17 mpg

Common Parts List 560SL, 1986–1989

Engine:

Oil filter	$8.00
Fuel filter	$42.50
Fuel pump(s)	$252.00 (two each)
Starter	$615 (rebuilt)
Alternator	$755.00
Radiator	$640.00
Fan clutch	$460.00
Water pump	$280.00

Body:

Front bumper:	
Bumper end—left	$97.00
Bumper end—right	$97.00
Bumper guard—left	$73.00
Bumper guard—right	$73.00
Bumper molding	$308.00
Hood	$2,060.00
Left front fender	$525.00
Rear bumper:	
Bumper end—left	$122.00
Bumper end—right	$122.00
Bumper guard—left	$42.00
Bumper guard—right	$42.00
Bumper molding	$308.00
Windshield	$1,023.00
Headlight assembly	$520.00
Taillight lens	$244.00

Exhaust:

Catalytic converter	$285.00 each (rebuilt)
Rear muffler	$346.00

Chassis:

Brake master	$252.00
Front rotor	$52.00 each
Front pads (set)	$77.00
Front shocks	$137.00 each
Rear shocks	$140.00 each

Fuel/fuel injection—The 1972 to 1974 models could use leaded or unleaded fuel. Early emissions controls affected performance, drivability, and gas mileage. Vapor lock caused hot-start problems. The 1975 and 1976 models suffered vapor lock more frequently because the catalytic converters were located in the engine compartment. The tight fit and lack of airflow often causes the fuel to boil and can result in vapor lock. The 1977 model's converters were relocated to under the car to resolve the vapor lock problems. The 1976 model's CIS fuel injection replaced the earlier electronic fuel injection.

Convertible top—Water can get trapped in the convertible top well and cause rust. Open it up to check the well and examine the condition of the top and the function of mechanicals.

Camshafts—Regular and frequent oil changes are a must. Failure to do this leads to premature wear of the camshafts, and the right side is usually the first to suffer. Be sure to have a mechanic pull the valve covers and check for wear.

Lower rear control arm mounting point for the front suspension—This was subject to cracking. In 1985 MBZ NA issued a recall to all 350/450 owners. Have this inspected by your mechanic because owners may not have had the recall fix applied.

Hardtop—Examine the condition of the electrical connector to the hardtop for damaged wiring or a damaged connector. This is easy to forget about when removing the hardtop.

Check that the VINs match. Look in the driver-side doorjamb for the VIN and build date and match it to the VIN stamped on the radiator support sheet metal and the left windshield pillar.

All Models:

Camshafts—Regular and frequent oil changes are a must. Failure to do this leads to premature wear of the camshafts, and the right side is usually the first to suffer. Have a mechanic pull the valve covers and check for wear.

Single- or double-row chains—In 1981 to 1983 380SL models, single-row chains tend to wear and stretch. If stretched, the chain can jump a tooth and result in valve-to-piston contact. Models from 1984 and on used double-row chains. Mercedes has discontinued sale of single-row chains, and engines are usually converted whenever a rebuild is done. It is expensive to perform, but much less expensive than a complete rebuild.

Timing chains—Replacement is recommended at 100,000-mile intervals. Plastic guides and banana rails should also be replaced at the same time. This project is labor intensive; expect to spend anywhere from $800 to $1,000.

Oil level sensor unit—This can leak where it passes through the engine block. The 3.8- and 4.5-liter V-8s are easier to change than the 5.6-liter, but all require removing the oil pan. The 560SL also requires dropping the front crossmember, which is expensive to fix.

Plastic tank radiators—Check for evidence of leaking. Over time, the plastic becomes brittle and the hose necks can break off.

Maintenance—Tune-ups should be done annually or every 15,000 miles. Check for fuel leaks at injectors and vacuum leaks. The rubber hoses get brittle over time and crack.

Rear control arm bushings—These deteriorate over time and cause vibration under acceleration.

Brake system—The fluid should be flushed annually because brake fluid attracts moisture and can lead to corrosion forming in master cylinder and calipers. If the corrosion is severe, it can result in brake-system failure.

Convertible top—Examine the top for cuts, tears, and mold. Replacement tops are readily available; however, expect to spend $1,200 to $1,800 for a replacement.

Fuel/fuel injection—The 1972 to 1974 models could use leaded or unleaded fuel. Early emissions controls affected performance, drivability, and gas mileage. Vapor lock caused hot-start problems. The 1975 and 1976 models suffered vapor lock more frequently because the catalytic converters were located in the engine compartment. A tight fit and lack of airflow causes the fuel to boil and can result in vapor lock. The 1977 model's converters were relocated under the car to resolve the vapor lock problems. The 1976 model's CIS fuel injection replaced the earlier electronic fuel injection.

Quarter vents—These vents on the SLC models deteriorate over time. Water can leak in and result in rust on the sheet metal below the vents and in the rear cowl areas.

Floorboards—Lift the floor mats to check for damp carpeting. Water can leak in, get trapped under carpeting, and cause the floorboards to rust.

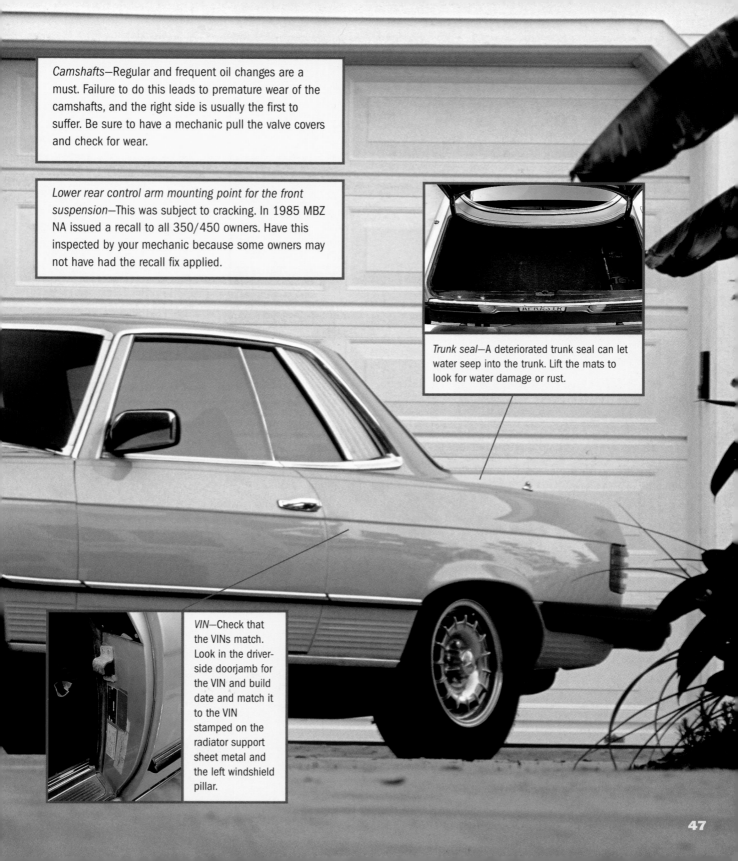

Camshafts—Regular and frequent oil changes are a must. Failure to do this leads to premature wear of the camshafts, and the right side is usually the first to suffer. Be sure to have a mechanic pull the valve covers and check for wear.

Lower rear control arm mounting point for the front suspension—This was subject to cracking. In 1985 MBZ NA issued a recall to all 350/450 owners. Have this inspected by your mechanic because some owners may not have had the recall fix applied.

Trunk seal—A deteriorated trunk seal can let water seep into the trunk. Lift the mats to look for water damage or rust.

VIN—Check that the VINs match. Look in the driver-side doorjamb for the VIN and build date and match it to the VIN stamped on the radiator support sheet metal and the left windshield pillar.

Garage Watch: 380SL/560SL

560SL

Plastic tank radiators—Check plastic tank radiators for evidence of leaking. Over time, the plastic becomes brittle and hose necks can break off.

560SL

Chin spoiler—Check the under-bumper chin spoiler for curb damage.

BOTH

Convertible top—Water can become trapped in the convertible top well and cause rust. Open it up to check closely and examine the condition of the top and the function of mechanicals. Examine the convertible top for cuts, tears, and mold. Replacement tops are readily available, but expect to spend $1,200 to $1,800 to replace it.

BOTH

Hardtop—Examine the condition of the electrical connector to the hardtop for damaged wiring or a damaged connector. This is easy to forget about when removing the hardtop.

BOTH

Trunk seal—A deteriorated trunk seal can let water seep into the trunk. Lift mats to look for water damage or rust.

BOTH

Floorboards—Lift the floor mats to check for damp carpeting. Water can leak in, become trapped under carpeting, and cause the floorboards to rust.

560SL

Camshafts—Regular and frequent oil changes are a must. Failure to do this leads to premature wear of the camshafts, and the right side is usually the first to suffer. Be sure to have a mechanic pull the valve covers and check for wear.

380SL

Chains—Have a mechanic remove the valve covers to check for single- or double-row chains in 1981 to 1983 380SLs. The single-row chains have a tendency to wear and stretch. If stretched, chains jump a tooth and result in valve-to-piston contact. The 1984 380SLs and later models used double-row chains. MBZ has discontinued the sale of the single-row chains, and engines are usually converted whenever a rebuild is done. This is expensive to perform, but much less expensive than a complete rebuild.

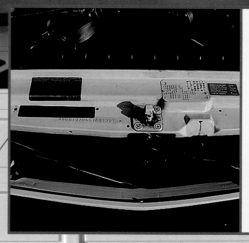

BOTH

VIN—Check that the VINs match. Look in the driver-side doorjamb for VIN and build date and match to the VIN stamped on the radiator support sheet metal and the left windshield pillar.

560SL

Power—The 1986 to 1989 560SL's 47 percent power increase solved the performance shortfall of the 380SL's smaller engine.

560SL

Oil level—Watch for evidence of the oil level sensor leaking. Repair involves dropping the front crossmember and suspension in order to remove the oil pan. This is expensive unless the leak is really bad, and it's probably best to live with it short term.

Chapter 3

R129 SLs: 1990–2002
Basic History

After a 17-year production run that saw EPA and DOT regulations change dramatically, the venerable W107 SL was long overdue for replacement. Development of a replacement had originally begun in the early 1970s, but it was delayed by the need to develop and introduce a small sedan, the 190, in late 1982.

By 1984, the new SL design had been settled on and development had resumed. The R129 chassis SL was introduced to the public at the 1989 Geneva show. The 300SL-24 and the 500SL went on sale in the United States in late 1989.

In 1991, the 6-liter V-12-powered 600SL was introduced. In 1992, the 300SL-24 received the larger 3.2-liter engine and became the 320SL.

Mercedes-Benz altered the badging of its entire model range for the 1994 model year and swapped the letters and numbers. For example, the 320SL became the SL320, and so on.

Coming from a design team headed by Bruno Sacco, the 1990 R129 SLs featured a neat aero-style look, along with many lessons that had been learned since the W107 chassis was introduced. Incorporating a wealth of safety innovations, the most innovative has to be the spring-loaded, pop-up roll bar. A complex set of sensors continuously monitors the car's attitude on the road, and when the sensors detect a predetermined level of instability, the roll bar is deployed to the upright position in 0.3 seconds. The roll bar can also be deployed manually (it takes 3 to 4 seconds) and functions with the tops in place or removed.

Microprocessor-controlled hydraulics are used to raise and lower the convertible soft top. The process takes about 30 seconds to complete and involves automatically lowering the windows (and roll bar if deployed), raising the rear soft window, opening the rear hatch, unlatching the top from the windshield header, folding the roof backward into its stowage well, closing the rear hatch, and raising the windows.

The removable hardtop weighs about 75 pounds and requires two people to remove it.

To protect the sides of the body from parking-lot damage or debris kicked up from the road, plastic cladding runs the length of the body between the front and rear wheels and below the beltline. On the early cars, this cladding is a complementary color, usually a metallic gray, and matches the color of the front and rear bumpers. On later cars, the bumpers and body cladding are the same color as the body.

The leather seats are electrically adjustable and include fore and aft, vertical, seat back recline, headrest adjustment, and three programmable memory settings. The shoulder belts are anchored to the seat, and the height of the belts is also electrically adjustable. The seats themselves feature cast-magnesium frames and are part of the overall passenger protection design and provide additional crush resistance in side impacts.

The steering wheel is adjustable for height and telescope. When the driver's door is opened, the steering wheel retracts and moves upward for easy entry and exit.

The external mirrors and inside rearview mirror are electrically operated, and the mirror positions can also be stored with the memory settings of the driver's seat.

A remote locking system provides security for the car and its contents. An infrared transmitter can communicate with the SL from as far away as 20 feet. When the car is locked or unlocked (either using the key or the remote control), the doors, trunk, fuel filler door, and the various cubbyholes in the interior are all locked.

The SL's climate control system has been simplified and can be preset to maintain temperature.

The R129 chassis has a 2.3-inch-longer wheelbase; however, the overall length is shorter by 4.3 inches because of the U.S. specification bumpers that were integrated with the design, rather than added. Track is increased 2.6 inches in front and 2.2 inches in the rear.

Suspension is derived from components used in both the 190 and 300 sedans with MacPherson struts, coil springs, and gas-pressure shocks up front. Rear suspension is the Mercedes-Benz five-arm multilink, coil springs, gas-pressure shocks with anti-lift and anti-squat geometry. While not included in the earliest cars, Adaptive Damping System (known as ADS) was added within a year of introduction. ADS automatically adjusts firmness based on several factors.

Steering is taken care of by a power-assisted recirculating ball system, and braking is done through two-circuit, hydraulic power-assisted, four-wheel disc brakes and ABS. The front rotors for the 300 and 500SL models are ventilated, while the rear rotors are solid. The 600SL uses ventilated front and rear rotors.

The engines offered included the 3.0-liter DOHC 24-valve inline six-cylinder in the 300SL-24 (up to 1991) and the 3.2-liter DOHC 24-valve inline six-cylinder from 1992 and later.

The 500SL/SL500 from 1989 to 1998 used an aluminum block and head DOHC V-8 with four valves per cylinder. The SL500 from 1999 on had an SOHC alloy block and head V-8 with three valves per cylinder.

The big news for 1991 was the release of a DOHC 90-degree V-12 with four valves per cylinder. This aluminum block/heads engine produced a whopping 420 foot-pounds of torque at 3,800 rpm. Distinguishing the 600SL/SL600 from the other models were discrete deck lid badging and small V-12 emblems on the front fenders. The front bumper is extended forward approximately 2 inches to provide additional accident crush room for the longer 12-cylinder engine.

The 300SL was available with a five-speed manual transmission, which was an unusual move from Mercedes. The automatic transmission was also a five-speed automatic. The SL320 used these same transmissions during its production run.

The V-8-powered cars were equipped with the four-speed automatic from introduction up to 1995. A five-speed automatic was standard equipment from 1996 on. The V-12 cars from 1991 to 1995 had a four-speed automatic. A five-speed automatic was standard from 1996 on.

Common problems to be aware of include a recall on 1997 SLs. In areas of the country that experience high humidity conditions, the moisture could cause the airbag ignition generator to corrode and deploy the airbag without warning. A recall was issued to have dealers replace the airbag module. Have a mechanic verify the fix was completed.

Cars equipped with the Brake Assist system may be subject to a recall announced in May 2004 that affects cars built after October 2001. Check the build date of the car and have a mechanic confirm if this recall applies.

The factory recommends extended oil change intervals. Mechanics strongly recommend changing the oil at 5,000- to 7,500-mile intervals. Stretching the oil changes can lead to increased wear of engine components and causes excessive build-up of sludge in the bottom of the oil pan.

Be sure to use only Mercedes-Benz engine coolant. Use of antifreeze (typically greenish in color) that is not specifically formulated for alloy engines can lead to corrosion inside the engine. Over time, this can lead to a variety of problems, like overheating and other, more serious, engine damage.

Mechanics have noticed an increase in brake light switch failures. The brake light switch is what illuminates the brake lights. The switch also turns off the cruise control when the brakes are applied and sends a signal to the Emergency Brake Assist system. A defective switch can cause a "Check Engine" light to illuminate, as well as other system faults. When replacing a bad switch, mechanics will need to diagnose and reset multiple systems.

Potential owners have several models to choose from. With older cars that have high mileage, be sure to have the car checked out by a knowledgeable mechanic. The ability to put the top down and drive will mean these cars will continue to be popular. Find the best one you can afford, remove the top, and enjoy.

Shown here is a 1994 SL320. Looking from the passenger side, the controls for seat adjustments are mounted in the door panels. The center dash vents are independently adjustable. The round opening in the lower outboard corner of the dash is a duct that feeds conditioned air into the door.

Behind the seats of this 1994 SL320 is a package shelf for items too large to fit in the trunk. The rollover bar has been manually deployed in this photo. The soft top is stowed beneath the upholstered cover and is raised or lowered by a switch in the center console.

Opposite: The dashboard-mounted VIN sticker is in the lower left corner of the windshield of the 1994 the SL320. Confirm that the VIN matches the VIN plate in doorjamb.

Above: Here is a rear view of a 1994 SL320. The ribbed taillight design helps keep the rear light lens clean. The rollover hoop has been manually deployed in this photo.

The updated steering wheel and airbag design lead a driver's eyes to the easy-to-read instrumentation in the 1998 SL500. The center console has multiple, lockable storage containers that are interconnected with the central locking system. Door-mounted controls for passenger-seat adjustments and memory settings are visible in this photo.

The area behind the seats of the 1998 SL500 is plushly carpeted. Two stowage containers offer additional room for personal items and are interconnected with the central locking system. The left one contains the CD player, and the circular speakers for the sound system are tucked in the outboard corners. The electrical plug for the removable top is visible in this photo.

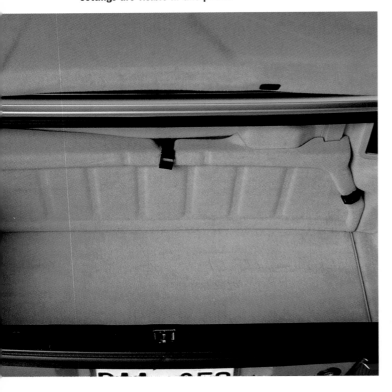

The R129 trunks for the 1998 SL500 are luxuriously appointed. Removable carpeting reveals a space-saver spare and jack. The detachable mesh windscreen is stowed behind the panel at the forward bulkhead.

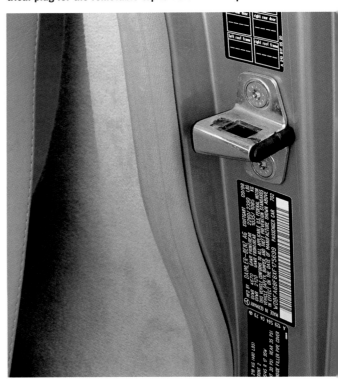

From top to bottom, the SRS airbag replacement sticker shows the location of the airbags and dates they should be replaced. The VIN sticker provides the VIN and build date, and the bottom sticker provides information on tire sizes and inflation. The VIN should match the one on the left front corner of the dash, which is visible through the windshield.

Make sure the VIN on the doorjamb sticker and VIN plate on the dash match. The electrical wire for the removable hardtop is visible at the 11:00 position, and the seatbelt mounted to the seat is at the 10:00 position.

The taillight design for the SL600 changed slightly from 1994 to 1995. The self-cleaning ribbing is more rounded, and the SL600 badging is discreet.

Common Parts List
R129 300SL, 1990–1993

Engine:

Oil filter	$9.75
Fuel filter	$42.50
Fuel pumps (two per car)	$252.00 each
Starter	$229 (rebuilt)
Alternator	$363.00 (rebuilt)
Radiator	$620.00
Fan clutch	$177.00
Water pump	$360.00

Body:

Front bumper	$1,330.00
Hood	$1,230.00
Left front fender	$282.00
Right rear quarter panel	$640.00
Rear bumper	$850.00
Windshield	$833.50
Headlight assembly	$280.00
Taillight lens	$155.00

Exhaust:

Catalytic converter	$3,760.00 (including front pipe)
Center muffler	$532.40
Rear muffler	$565.00
Oxygen sensor	$203.37

Chassis:

Brake master	$252.00
Front rotor	$83.00 each
Front pads (set)	$83.00
Front shocks	$260.00 each
Rear shocks:	
Standard	$152.00
Self-leveling	$505.00

Common Parts List
R129 SL320, 1995–1997

Engine:

Oil filter	$9.75
Fuel filter	$42.50
Fuel pumps (two per car)	$252.00 each
Starter	$222 (rebuilt)
Alternator	$338.00 (rebuilt)
Radiator	$665.00
Fan clutch	$177.00
Water pump	$262.00

Body:

Front bumper:	
up to 1995	$1,330.00
1996–1997	$1,220.00
w/AMG pkg from 1996	$1,700.00
Hood	$1,230.00
Left front fender	$282.00
Right rear quarter panel	$640.00
Rear bumper	$850.00
Windshield	$833.50
Headlight assembly	
through 1994: w/o turn signal	$280.00
1995-on: standard	$332.00
Gas discharge (Xenon):	$1,480.00
Taillight lens	$155.00

Exhaust:

Catalytic converter	$2,250.00 (including front pipe)
Center muffler	$532.40
Rear muffler	$565.00
Oxygen sensor	
up to 1995	$202.53
from 1995–on	$157.00

Chassis:

Brake master	$252.00
Front rotor	$83.00 each
Front pads (set)	$83.00
Front shocks	$244.00 each
Rear shocks:	
Standard	$152.00 each
Self-leveling	$505.00 each

Rating Chart
R129 SLs, 1990–2002

Model	Comfort/ Amenities	Reliability	Collectibility	Parts/Service	Est. Annual Repair Costs
300SL	★★★	★★★⸼	★★★⸼	★★★⸼	★★★
SL320	★★★★	★★★⸼	★★★⸼	★★★⸼	★★★
500SL/SL500	★★★★	★★★⸼	★★★⸼	★★★⸼	★★★★
600SL/SL600	★★★★⸼	★★★⸼	★★★⸼	★★★⸼	★★★★

Technical Specifications:
R129 300SL/SL320, 1989–1997

Engine:

Type	Inline six, DOHC, four valves per cylinder
Displacement cc/ci:	
300SL	2,962/180.6
SL320	3,199/195.0
Compression ratio:	
300SL	10.0:1
SL320	10.0:1
Bhp @ rpm:	
300SL	228 @ 6,300
SL320	228 @ 5,600
Torque ft-lb @ rpm:	
300SL	201 @ 4,600
SL320	232 @ 3,750
Injection type:	
300SL	Bosch electronic
SL320	HFM fully electronic fuel injection/ignition w/anti-knock control
Fuel requirement	Premium unleaded

Chassis/drivetrain:

Transmission:	
Automatic	Five-speed
Manual (opt. 300SL)	Five-speed
Steering	Recirculating ball, power-assist
Front suspension	Unequal-length A-arms, coil springs, tube shocks, anti-roll bar
Rear suspension	Independent five-arm multilink, coil springs, tube shocks, anti-lift and anti-squat geometry
Differential:	
Automatic	3.69:1
Manual (optional)	3.46:1

General:

Wheelbase	99.0
Weight:	
300SL	4,035
SL320	4,010
Wheels	16x8 H2 aluminum alloy
Tires	225/55ZR-16
Brake system:	two-circuit hydraulic power-assisted four-wheel discs w/ABS
Front	11.8-inch vented discs
Rear	10.9-inch solid discs
0–60 mph	10.5 sec
Maximum speed mph	149
Fuel economy:	city/hwy
EPA estimated mpg	15/22

Common Parts List
R129 500SL/SL500, 1990–2002

Engine:

Oil filter	$13.00
Fuel filter	$42.50
Fuel pumps (two per car)	$252.00 each
Starter	$254.50 (rebuilt)
Alternator	$627.00 (rebuilt)
Radiator	$565.00
Fan clutch	$560.00
Water pump	$418.00

Body:

Front bumper:	
through 1995	$1,330.00
1996–on	$1,220.00
w/AMG styling pkg	$1,700.00
Hood	$1,230.00
Left front fender	$282.00
Right rear quarter panel	$640.00
Rear bumper	$850.00
Windshield	$833.50
Headlight assembly:	
through 1994: w/o turn signal:	$280.00
1995–on: standard	$332.00
Gas discharge (Xenon)	$1,480.00
Taillight lens	$155.00

Exhaust:

Catalytic converter	
Left side	$1150.00
Right side	$1150.00
Center muffler	$532.40
Rear muffler	$565.00
Oxygen sensor	
Up to 1995	$172.70
1996–on:	
Before catalyst, left	$157.00
Before catalyst, right	$139.00
Diagnostic probe (two per car)	$172.70 (each)

Chassis:

Brake master:	
through 1997	$252.00
1998–on	$346.00
Front rotor	$83.00 each
Front pads (set)	$83.00
Front shocks	$260.00 each
Rear shocks:	
Standard	$152.00
Self-leveling	$505.00

Technical Specifications:
R129 500SL/SL500, 1989–2002

Engine:

Type:

500SL/SL500 to 1998	DOHC, V-8, four valves per cylinder, aluminum block/heads
SL500 from 1999	SOHC V-8, three valves per cylinder, alloy block/heads

Displacement cc/ci:

500SL/SL500 to 1998	4,973/303.5
SL500 from 1999	4,966/

Compression ratio:

500SL/SL500 to 1998	11.0:1
SL500 from 1999	10.0:1

Bhp @ rpm:

500SL/SL500 to 1998	315 @ 5,600
SL500 from 1999	302 @ 5,600

Torque ft-lb @ rpm:

500SL/SL500 to 1998	347 @ 3,900
SL500 from 1999	339 @ 2,700–4,250
Injection type	Electronic fuel injection
Fuel requirement	Premium unleaded, 91 octane

Chassis/drivetrain:

Transmission:

500SL/SL500	Four-speed electronically controlled automatic
SL500 (1996-on)	Five-speed driver-adaptive electronic automatic
Steering	Recirculating ball, power-assist
Front suspension	Modified MacPherson struts, lower A-arms, coil springs, tube shocks, anti-roll bar
Rear suspension	Independent five-arm multilink, coil springs, tube shocks, anti-lift and anti-squat geometry
Differential	2.65:1

General:

Wheelbase	99.0
Weight	4,160

Wheels:

to 1998	16x8.0J H2 aluminum alloy
1999–2000	17x8.25J aluminum alloy, five-hole design
optional sport pkg.	18x8.0J fr/18x9.0J rear, AMG design
2001	18x8.5J fr/18x9.5J rear, aluminum alloy
2002	18x8.5J fr/18x9.5J rear, aluminum alloy
avail. on request	17x8.25J, five-slot design

Tires:

to 1998	225/55ZR-16
1999–2000	245/45ZR17 performance rated
optional sport pkg.	245/40ZR18 fr/275/35ZR18 rear
2001	245/40ZR18 fr/275/35ZR18 rear
2002	245/40ZR18 fr/275/35ZR18 rear
avail. on request	245/45WR17

Brake system:	two-circuit hydraulic power assist four-wheel discs w/ABS
Front	11.8-inch vented discs
Rear	10.9-inch solid discs

0–60 mph:

500SL/SL500 to 1998	6.4 sec
SL500 from 1999	6.1 sec
Maximum speed mph	155 (electronically limited)

Fuel economy: city/hwy

EPA estimated mpg

500SL/SL500 to 1998	14/18
SL500 from 1999	16/23

Technical Specifications: R129 600SL/SL600, 1993–2002

Engine:

Type	DOHC, V-12, four valves per cylinder, aluminum block/heads
Displacement cc/ci	5,987/365.4
Compression ratio	10.0:1
Bhp @ rpm	389 @ 5,200
Torque ft-lb @ rpm	420 @ 3,800
Injection type	ME 1.0 fully electronic fuel injection
Fuel requirement	Premium unleaded, 91 octane

Chassis/drivetrain:

Transmission:	
to 1995	Four-speed electronically controlled automatic w/ASR
From 1996–on:	Five-speed electronically controlled automatic w/driver-adaptive control
Steering	Recirculating ball, w/speed-sensitive power assist
Front suspension	Modified MacPherson struts, lower A-arms, coil springs, tube shocks, anti-roll bar. Adaptive Damping System (ADS) w/selectable ride height
Rear suspension	Independent five-arm multilink, coil springs, tube shocks, anti-lift and anti-squat geometry. Adaptive Damping System (ADS) w/s electable ride height.
Differential	2.65:1

General:

Wheelbase	99.0
Weight	4,615
Wheels:	
to 1998	16x8.0J H2 aluminum alloy
optional	18x8.0J fr/18x9.0J rear
1999	17x8.25J aluminum alloy, five-hole design
optional sport pkg.	18x8.0J fr/18x9.0J rear, AMG design
2000	17x8.25J aluminum alloy, five-hole design
optional sport pkg.	18x8.5J fr/18x9.5J rear, aluminum alloy
2001	18x8.5J fr/18x10.0J rear, two-piece aluminum alloy
2002	18x8.5J fr/18x10.0J rear, two-piece aluminum alloy
avail on request	17x8.25J, five-hole design
Tires:	
to 1998	225/55ZR-16
optional	245/40ZR18 fr/275/35ZR18 rear
1999	245/45ZR17 performance rated
optional sport pkg.	245/40ZR18 fr/275/35ZR18 rear
2000	245/45ZR17 performance rated
optional sport pkg.	245/40ZR18 fr/275/35ZR18 rear
2001	245/40ZR18 fr/275/35ZR18 rear
2002	245/40ZR18 fr/275/35ZR18 rear
avail. on request	245/45WR17
Brake system:	two-circuit hydraulic power-assisted four-wheel disc w/ABS
Front	11.8-inch vented discs
Rear	10.9-inch solid discs
0 – 60 mph	6.0
Maximum speed mph	155 (electronically limited)
Fuel economy:	city/hwy
EPA estimated mpg:	13/18

Common Parts List
R129 600SL/ SL600, 1993–2002

Engine:

Oil filter	$21.50
Fuel filter	$42.50
Fuel pumps (two per car)	$252.00 each
Starter	$255.56
Alternator	$490.00 (rebuilt)
Radiator	$795.00
Fan clutch	$640.00
Water pump	$500.00

Body:

Front bumper	$1,700.00
Hood	$1,230.00
Left front fender	$282.00
Right rear quarter panel	$640.00
Rear bumper:	$850.00
AMG style, from 1999:	1,860.00
Windshield:	$833.50
Headlight assembly	
up to 1994: w/o turn signal	$280.00
1995-on: standard	$332.00
Gas discharge (Xenon)	$1,480.00
Taillight lens:	
to 6/1998	$155.00
from 7/1998-on	$156.00

Exhaust:

Catalytic converter:	
Left	$1,170.00
Right	$1,170.00
Muffler (two per car)	$1,050.00 each
Front pipe (left and right)	$159.00 each
Tailpipe extension	$153.00
Oxygen sensor:	
To 1995 (two per car)	$202.53 each
1996–2001 (four per car)	$172.70 each

Chassis:

Brake master	$1,460.00
Front rotor	$100.00 each
Front pads (set)	
thru 6/1998	$83.00
from 7/1998	$95.00
Front shocks	$628.69 each
Rear shocks	$505.00 each

Garage Watch: 300SL/SL320

Water pumps—Look for leaking water pumps. The replacement will cost $280 for the part plus about three hours of labor to remove and replace the water pump.

Timing cover leaks—Pull the black plastic cover at the front of the valve cover and examine it closely. Watch for oil leaking down to the alternator. It usually traces back to front timing cover leaks. The part is about $40 and one and a half to two hours to replace.

Oil leaks—Look for oil leaks on the right side of the engine block. This may be an indication of a bad head gasket. A replacement part is not all that expensive, but the repair will take between six and eight hours of labor.

Power steering pumps—Check the pump for evidence of leaks. The best way to check is from underneath. Look for moisture in, around, and on the pump. New pumps cost more than $1,200. Kits are available to reseal the pumps, and figure about four to five hours of labor plus parts. The power steering pump provides pressure for both systems on cars with self-leveling suspension. In that situation, repairs take longer and cost even more money.

Dipstick—Check the color of the dipstick. If it is dark colored and has deposits, it indicates a lack of oil changes or possible overheating. If it is clean and clear, it indicates regular oil changes or recent dipstick replacement.

Oil filler cap—Look inside the cap at the rocker. Is it aluminum colored? If so, this indicates regular oil changes. If it is reddish-brown, it confirms dipstick discoloration, which means the oil wasn't changed regularly and the engine overheated.

Airflow sensor wiring harnesses—The wiring harness that connects to the airflow sensor(s) is in an area where engine heat will cause insulation to dry out and disintegrate. Make sure a mechanic checks for deteriorated insulation. Don't do it yourself because you may cause further damage and problems. A replacement harness is about $500 and two hours of labor to replace.

Defective smog pump—This is more noticeable when the engine is cold because it will be noisy. Once the operating temp is reached, it will quiet down. Noise is a sign that it needs replacing.

500SL/SL500

Head gaskets—Gaskets are good for up to 100,000 miles. At that point, begin watching for signs of possible head gasket replacements.

500SL/SL500

Door pockets—The door pockets, especially those on the driver-side door, have a tendency to break. They can be fixed by removing the door panel, and where the pocket's plastic pins have broken, a washer and sheet-metal screw can be used to secure the pocket in place.

ALL MODELS

Fuel-injection wiring harnesses—From 1992 on, engine heat causes insulation to prematurely dry out, crack, and disintegrate. This can begin at the 50,000- to 60,000-mile mark, and by 100,000 it is usually severe. Be mindful of these because bad insulation may result in wires shorting out, which can damage engine computers. Harnesses are between $350 to $800, depending on the car. Leave this one to a qualified mechanic.

500SL/SL500

Valve cover gaskets—Look for leaking valve cover gaskets. This is common and they are fairly easy to replace.

500SL/SL500

Ticking/tapping from engine—Raise the hood and listen for tapping or ticking from the engine's top end. This may indicate the plastic oil supply tubes for rockers have become dislodged. Have these checked as soon as it is practical. It is not that hard to fix, and you save money by replacing them as soon as you can. Fix leaky valve cover gaskets at the same time.

500SL/SL500

Fan belt tensioners—
Tensioners should be checked at regular intervals. Check service receipts to see if and when this may have been done. If it hasn't, have them replaced as soon as it is practical.

ALL MODELS

*Lower control arms—*The lower control arm bushings wear out over time. Have these checked by a mechanic.

*Driveshaft flex disc—*The rubber flex discs are subject to cracking. Have a mechanic check the condition. Also check the condition of the driveshaft, support bearings, and U-joints.

*Front upper shock mounts—*Check these for cracking and tearing. If they are bad enough, gas-pressurized shocks can rotate and may come through the rubber mount. This will usually will leave an "outie" divot in the hood just above the shock mount.

ALL MODELS

*Power steering pumps—*Check the pump for evidence of leaking. The best way to check is from underneath. Look for moisture in, around, and on the pump. Four different pumps were used and can cost more than $1,200 to replace. Kits are available to reseal the pumps, so figure six to eight hours of labor plus parts. On cars with self-leveling suspensions, the power steering pump provides pressure for both systems. Repairs take longer and are more expensive.

600SL/SL600

*Fuel lines—*Check for fuel lines that have become brittle with age. High underhood temps tend to dry everything out and can cause hoses and electrical lines to become brittle.

Chapter 4

R170 SLK230/ SLK320/SLK32 AMG: 1998–2004
Basic History

Introduced to the world at the 1996 Turin show, the R170 hit showrooms in late 1997. The two-seater was based on the C-class platform and designed by a team working under the direction of Bruno Sacco. Resembling a wedge from the side, the SLK230 featured a two-piece steel-folding roof that takes about 25 seconds to retract into the rear deck.

The SLK is 19.8 inches shorter and 1,200 pounds lighter than the SL-series roadsters. It came into market to compete with cars like the BMW Z3, Honda S2000, Mazda Miata, Toyota MR2, and Audi TT.

Powered by a derivative of the C-class sedan engine, the 2.3-liter DOHC four-valve-per-cylinder inline-four used a belt-driven supercharger with a liquid-to-air intercooler that raised power to 185 brake horsepower and 200 foot-pounds of torque. The SLK was capable of 0-to-60-mile-per-hour times of 7.2 seconds, so its performance was impressive but hampered by the five-speed electronically controlled automatic.

The suspension was based on C-class components with independent double wishbones in front and a five-arm multilink rear suspension. Coil springs, anti-roll bars, anti-dive geometry, and gas pressure shocks were used to complete the platform.

Brake components from the larger E-class sedans had ventilated rotors in front and solid rotors in back. Power-assisted ABS with Brake Assist was standard. The recirculating ball steering came with power assist and a hydraulic damper.

It did not take long for the public to accept the SLK, and in less than a year, Mercedes-Benz offered enhancements to make the package even more desirable. A five-speed manual gearbox was introduced in 1999, which made the SLK230 the first U.S. specification Mercedes-Benz available with a manual transmission in many years.

In 2001, power output of the four-cylinder was raised to 192 brake horsepower, a six-speed manual gearbox replaced the five-speed, and the V-6-powered SLK320 was introduced. Along with the 3.2-liter engine, a minor exterior restyle in 2001 featured body-colored trim, revised bumpers, sill extensions, and turn-signal repeaters on the outside rearview mirrors. The trunk release was relocated to the top edge of the license plate surround. Taillights received clear strips for back-up lights and turn signals to complete the new look.

The SLK32 AMG arrived in 2002 and sported a super-charged V-6, SpeedShift five-speed automatic, AMG sport-tuned suspension, wider AMG wheels, and larger brakes to match the increased power. With 340 horsepower on tap from the engine and 0-to-60-mile-per-hour times in the mid-four-second range, the SLK was now a serious performer.

Cosmetic changes in 2002 included a restyled front air dam, black mesh air intakes, side skirts, and a revised rear bumper. A color-keyed spoiler on top of the rear deck, dual polished stainless-steel exhaust pipes, and a revised rear apron let others know this SLK meant business.

Without question, the unique retractable hardtop sets the SLK apart from the competition. It takes approximately 25 seconds to transform from top up to an open-air road-ster. The two hinged panels are operated by a hydraulic pump that provides pressure to five slave cylinders—two operate the rear deck, two more operate the top, and one locks and unlocks the latching mechanisms at the wind-shield header. The trunk capacity is 9.5 cubic feet when the top is up. With the top retracted, this is reduced down to 3.6 cubic feet, which doesn't leave much room for luggage.

Occupants are treated to leather-covered seats, CFC-free air conditioning, dual temperature controls, and electrostatic dust filters. Power windows, door locks, mirrors, and cruise control are standard equipment. The SLK230 has six-way, manually adjustable seats. Heated seats were optional. The SLK320 received eight-way electrical seating, polished wood trim, and a telescopic steering column. The SLK32 AMG offers heated sports seats and a leather-trimmed sport steering wheel and shift knob as standard equipment.

Tubular steel hoops are located immediately behind both seats that work in concert with the reinforced A-pillars to protect occupants in the event of a rollover. Driver and passenger airbags are standard. A BabySmart child seat system automatically deactivates the passenger airbag when a special seat is used. A sophisticated antitheft system protects the vehicle and personal belongings.

Options on the SLK230 included metallic paint, heated seats, trunk-mounted CD-changer, integrated phone, and a sports package with bigger wheels and tires.

Traction control, known as Automatic Slip Control (ASR), senses rear-wheel spin and applies a slight amount of rear-wheel braking to regain traction. If excessive wheel spin is detected, engine power is reduced. Electronic Stability Program (ESP) uses a series of inputs to help correct understeer and oversteer conditions, employing the ASR logic, by either applying brake force or reducing engine power until control is regained.

When running, the four-cylinder is somewhat noisy. The automatic-equipped cars feel a bit less sporty, but for those driving in stop-and-go traffic, the automatic may be the better choice.

With the top down, luggage space is greatly reduced, so pack light. The interior storage space is also limited. Tall drivers may find themselves cramped, and for some, this will be reminiscent of the early British sports cars. The seat-back adjusters are in an awkward position on the inboard side of the seat backs, up near the top.

Later on, the complex and complicated mechanisms for the retractable top could become a maintenance problem if adjustments are needed. Be sure to cycle the top to confirm that it functions properly.

There were two limited-production versions of this vehicle series offered. In 2000 there was a Limited Edition model that featured special interior trim and was available only in black. In 2004, the Special Edition was an end-of-model

limited-production run that included 17-inch wheels, Nappa leather on the seats and roll bars, rear spoiler, exterior chrome accents, and a painted front grille.

With a production run of more than 300,000 SLKs, there are plenty to choose from. A new model, the R171, was released in 2005, so there may be a good number of pre-owned SLKs to choose from.

The SRS, VIN, and tire stickers are located in left doorjamb. The VIN should match the one located on the left forward corner of the dash and the one stamped on the firewall.

This trunk has a capacity of 9.5 cubic feet with the top up and 3.6 cubic feet with the top down. The CD changer is located in the right corner. Check for any moisture under the carpeting. It could be a sign that the seals around the trunk lid may leak.

This is the 2004 SLK230 Special Edition engine. Supercharged and intercooled, the 2.3-liter DOHC four-cylinder is known to be noisy and a bit rough running. Automatic-equipped cars will be less spirited than manual transmission cars.

This 3.2-liter V-6 fills up the engine bay of the SLK320. Check for any leaks and examine the radiators and hoses for leaking. Look on the firewall for the VIN and compare it with the VIN on the sticker in the driver's doorjamb and on the dashboard.

This 2004 SLK230 Special Edition model signifies its last year of production. The wheels, paint, and interior colors are unique to the Special Edition.

The AMG engines are hand-assembled and have an engraved plaque on top of the intake plenum with the name of the individual who built the engine.

Looking over the driver's shoulder, the gauges have white faces, and the AMG logo is in the lower center of the speedometer.

Here is another view of the retracted hardtop. While the trunk space is reduced, everything fits neatly.

The SRS, VIN, and tire pressure stickers in the driver's doorjamb provide information. Make sure the VIN matches the dash-mounted sticker and the one in the center of the firewall.

Common Parts List
R170 SLK230, 1998–2004

Engine:

Oil filter	$9.75
Fuel filter	$38.00
Fuel pump(s)	$197.00
Starter	$316.00 (rebuilt)
Alternator (90 amp)	$286.50 (rebuilt)
Radiator	$462.00
Fan clutch	$215.43
Water pump	$184.00

Body:

Front bumper:	
1997–1999	$394.00
2000–2004	$288.00
AMG style w/o headlight washers	$1,670.00
AMG style w/headlight washers	$1,700.00
Hood	$555.00
Left front fender	$306.00
Right rear quarter panel	$505.00
Rear bumper	$488.00
Windshield:	
Standard tint	$378.00
Green/green tint	$655.40
Headlight assembly	$330.00
Taillight lens	$122.00

Exhaust:

Catalytic converter (including front pipe)	$2,040.00 (rebuilt)
Rear muffler	$372.00
Oxygen sensor:	
Before catalyst	$202.52
To 1999 (front)	$172.00
From 2000 (front)	$151.00

Chassis:

Brake master	$214.00
Front rotor	$47.50 each
Front pads (set)	$65.00
Front shocks:	
Standard	$157.00 each
Sport setting	$136.00 each
Rear shocks:	
Standard	$127.16 each
Sport setting	$136.00 each

Rating Chart
R170 SLK230/SLK320/SLK32 AMG, 1998–2004

Model	Comfort/Amenities	Reliability	Collectibility	Parts/Service Availability	Est. Annual Repair Costs
SLK230	★★★	★★★	★★★	★★★⯪	★★★
SLK320	★★★	★★★	★★★	★★★⯪	★★★
SLK32AMG	★★★	★★★	★★★⯪	★★★⯪	★★★

Technical Specifications:
R170 SLK230, 1998–2004

Engine:

Type	Supercharged, I-4, DOHC, four valves/cylinder
Displacement cc/ci	2,295/140
Compression ratio:	
1998–2000	8.8:1
2001–on	9.0:1
Bhp @ rpm:	
1998–2000	185 @ 5,300
2001–on	192 @ 5,300
Torque ft-lb @ rpm	200 @ 2,500
Injection type	Electronic, sequential port
Fuel requirement	Premium unleaded, 91 octane

Chassis/drivetrain:

Transmission:	
1998–2001	Five-speed electronically controlled automatic
Optional:	
1999–on	Five-speed manual
2002–on	Six-speed manual (standard)
Steering	Recirculating ball, hydraulic power-assist
Front suspension	Double wishbone, coil springs, gas-charged shocks, anti-roll bar
Rear suspension	Five-link, coil springs, gas-charged shocks, anti-roll bar, anti-lift and anti-squat geometry
Differential	3.27:1

General:

Wheelbase:	94.5
Weight:	
Automatic	3,110
Manual	3,055
Wheels:	
Standard	Alloy, 16x7.0 fr/16x8.0 rear
Optional	Alloy, 17x7.5 fr/17x8.5 rear
Tires:	
Standard	205/55R16 fr/225/50Rx16 rear
Optional	225/45ZR17 fr/245/40ZR17 rear
Brake system:	Four-wheel disc, vacuum-assist, ABS
Front	11.3-inch vented discs
Rear	10.9-inch solid discs
0–60 mph:	
Automatic	7.0 sec
Manual	6.9 sec
Maximum speed mph	130 (electronically limited)
Fuel capacity	15.9
Fuel economy:	
EPA estimated mpg:	city/highway
Automatic	23/30
Manual	20/29

Common Parts List
R170 SLK320, 2002–2004

Engine:

Oil filter	$18.50
Fuel filter	$109.00
Fuel pump(s)	$197.00
Starter	$253.75 (rebuilt)
Alternator	$215.00 (rebuilt)
Radiator	$302.00
Water pump	$360.00

Body:

Front bumper:	$288.99
AMG style w/o headlight washers:	$1,670.00
AMG style w/headlight washers:	$1,700.00
Hood:	$555.00
Left front fender:	$252.00
Right rear quarter panel:	$505.00
Rear bumper:	
w/sport pkg.:	
1998–1999	$360.00
2000–on	$308.00

Windshield:

Standard tint	$378.00
Green/green tint	$665.40
Headlight assembly:	
Standard	$330.00
Xenon gas discharge	$1,300.00
Taillight lens	$122.00

Exhaust:

Oxygen sensor:	
Front:	
Left	$1559.00
Right	$165.00
Rear	$168.00

Chassis:

Front rotor	$75.00 each
Front pads (set)	$72.00
Front shocks	$136.00 each
Rear shocks	$136.00 each

Technical specifications: R170 SLK320, 2001–2004

Engine:

Type	90-degree V-6, chain-driven SOHC per bank, two intake valves/one exhaust valve per cylinder
Displacement cc/ci	3199/195
Compression ratio	10.0:1
Bhp @ rpm:	215 @ 5,700
Torque ft-lb @ rpm:	221 @ 3,000–4,600
Injection type:	Electronic, sequential port
Fuel requirement:	Premium unleaded, 91 pump octane

Chassis/drivetrain:

Transmission:	
Standard	Six-speed manual
Optional	Five-speed electronically controlled automatic w/driver-adaptive shift logic
Steering	recirculating ball, hydraulic power-assist
Front suspension	Double wishbone, coil springs, gas-charged shocks, anti-roll bar
Rear suspension	Five-link, coil springs, gas-charged shocks, anti-roll bar, anti-lift and anti-squat geometry
Differential	3.27:1

General:

Wheelbase	94.5
Weight:	
Automatic	3,154
Manual	3,099
Wheels:	
Standard	Alloy, 16x7.0 fr/16x8.0 rear
Optional	Alloy, 17x7.5 fr/17x8.5 rear
Tires:	
Standard	205/55R16 fr/225/50x16 rear
Optional	225/45ZR17 fr/245/40ZR17 rear
Brake system:	Four-wheel disc, vacuum-assist, ABS
Front	11.8-inch vented discs
Rear	10.9-inch solid discs
0–60 mph:	
Automatic	6.6 sec
Manual	6.6 sec
Maximum speed mph	140 (est.)
Fuel capacity	15.9
EPA estimated mpg:	city/highway
Automatic	21/27
Manual	18/27

Common Parts List—R170 SLK32 AMG, 2002–2004

Engine:

Oil filter	$18.50
Fuel filter	$109.00
Fuel pump(s)	$197.00
Starter	$253.75 (rebuilt)
Alternator	$215.00 (rebuilt)
Radiator	$302.00
Water pump	$360.00

Body:

Front bumper:	
AMG-style w/o headlight washers	$1,670.00
AMG-style w/headlight washers	$1,700.00
Hood	$555.00
Left front fender	$252.00
Right rear quarter panel	$505.00
Rear bumper:	
w/sport pkg.:	
1998–1999	$360.00
2000–on	$308.00

Windshield:	
Standard tint	$378.00
Green/green tint $	665.40
Headlight assembly:	
Standard	$330.00
Xenon gas discharge	$1,300.00
Taillight lens	$102.00

Exhaust:

Oxygen sensor:	
Front:	
Left	$159.00
Right	$165.00
Rear	$165.00

Chassis:

Front rotor	$87.00 each
Front pads (set)	$75.00
Front shocks	$136.00 each
Rear shocks	$136.00 each

Technical specifications: R170 SLK32 AMG, 2002–2004

Engine:

Type	90-degree V-6, screw-type inter cooled supercharger, chain-driven SOHC per bank, two intake valves/one exhaust valve per cylinder
Displacement cc/ci	3,199/195
Compression ratio	9.0:1
Bhp @ rpm	349 @ 6,100
Torque ft-lb @ rpm	332 @ 3,000–4,600
Injection type	Electronic, sequential port
Fuel requirement	Premium unleaded, 91 pump octane

Chassis/drivetrain:

Transmission	AMG SpeedShift five-speed electronically controlled automatic w/driver-adaptive shift logic
Steering	Recirculating ball, Hydraulic power-assist

Front suspension	Double wishbone, coil springs, gas-charged shocks, anti-roll bar
Rear suspension	Five-link, coil springs, gas-charged shocks, anti-roll bar, anti-lift, and anti-squat geometry
Differential	3.07:1

General:

Wheelbase	94.5
Weight	3,220
Wheels	Alloy, 17x7.5 fr/17x8.5 rear
Tires	225/45ZR17 fr/245/40ZR17 rear
Brake system:	Four-wheel disc, vacuum-assist, ABS
Front	13.0-inch vented discs
Rear	11.8-inch solid discs
0–60 mph	4.8 sec
Maximum speed mph	155 electronically limited
Fuel capacity	15.9
Fuel economy:	
EPA estimated mpg	18 city/24 hwy

C-pillar—Look closely at both C-pillars, near the halfway point, for evidence of paint damage. The C-pillars may touch the trunk inner panels and cause damage to the paint. Some owners have used self-adhesive felt pads on trunk panels to help protect the paint.

Lightbulbs—These bulbs tend to burn out prematurely. It is often a taillight, which will activate a warning message. Check for loose or improperly fitting bulb sockets. Moisture may have caused corrosion in the socket. Cleaning and replacing bulbs may take care of the problem.

Fuel gauge—The common symptom is a gauge reading 7/8 full post-fill up. This may be a faulty gauge or a problem with the sending unit in the tank.

Electrical systems—Make sure all the electrical accessories and systems work, including the power windows, electric mirrors, seat adjusters, radio, lights, and turn signals. Open and close the top to make sure everything functions.

Some SLK320s have experienced a rough idle. It could be the engine ECU. If so, it can be replaced with an updated unit. Refer to the Service Bulletin 121/P-BB0765/14 ECU update.

Seat heaters—The seat heaters not functioning seems to occur more frequently with the SLK32AMG. Their seats are a different design from other SLK models. Be sure to check that the seat bottom heaters are working.

Dash and center console—Look for the color peeling off the dashboard or center console. The dash and console can be redyed and matched. Replacing pieces is expensive, and the replacements may eventually experience the same problem.

A rattling noise is from the exhaust system and happens between 1,000 and 2,500 rpm when the car is cold and under load, such as when the car is accelerating. Catalytic converters are close together and may be touching. The noise will go away as the car and exhaust system come up to operating temperatures.

There have been reports of knocking/thumping noise coming from behind the passenger seat. The noise is most noticeable when the top is up. An emission control system valve located behind the passenger seat is the culprit. This is not a serious problem; however, some of the early SLK320s can have this valve updated, which may reduce the noise. Refer to "Service Bulletin 103/P-B 47.30/15 Shut Off Valve."

Wind noise—As seals age, there may be some wind noise around the quarter windows. This could also be an indication of the top or windows being slightly out of alignment. Adjustments should be done by qualified service facilities, not by you.

Chapter 5

W111/112: 1960–1972
Basic History

Styled by Paul Bracq, the W111 chassis 220SEb was first shown at the 1961 Geneva show, and production of the coupe began shortly thereafter. The convertible version was announced at the 1961 Frankfurt show, and production of the convertible commenced in September 1961.

The coupe and convertible bodies were based on the W111 and W112 sedan platforms and were unique and did not share any panels with the sedan. The two-door models received quite a bit of hand finishing on the production lines, which explained their higher cost. The fit and finish of these two cars was superior to the sedans. Mechanically, a lot of components were shared with the sedans. The items shared included engines, transmissions, and suspensions.

The higher-end 300SE was introduced in February 1962 and ended production in December 1967. It was a low-volume car, and the largest year of production was 1965, which saw just over 700 cars built. Total production during five years was a little over 3,100.

The 300SE featured an all-alloy 3-liter engine and air suspension. Although it shared the body and major components of the 220SEb, Mercedes-Benz assigned it the W112 designation of the similarly powered sedans. A full-length chrome trim strip and wheel arch highlights identify the 3-liter as the top-of-the-line luxury model during the late 1960s.

Other minor differences separated the two models. A speedometer with higher top speed, the use of burr walnut wood in place of plain walnut on the dash, and a courtesy light delay feature were subtle changes. An upgraded rear axle design, larger disc brakes, and 14-inch wheels (to fit over the larger discs) were new for 1964.

In late 1965, the 250SE replaced the 2.2-liter model. Using the 2.5-liter engine from the then newly released S-class sedans, it had the same wheels (14-inch) as the 300SE, but it did not have the air suspension or additional chrome trim.

Production of the 250SE lasted just over two years, through December 1967, with approximately 6,000 cars produced. The 2.5-liter engine was known for high oil consumption and noisy valves. The development of an entirely new 2.8-liter engine was under way, and the new engine's availability marked the end of the 250SE model run.

During the 11-year production run, several engine capacities were used, beginning with the 2.2-liter, inline six cylinder brought over from the 220SE sedan. Performance with the 2,195-cc six was adequate considering the extra weight of the coupe and convertible.

The 300SE was fitted with an all-alloy 3-liter SOHC six-cylinder. Weighing in about 90 pounds less than the 3-liter iron block used in the sedans, the alloy cylinder block had press-fit dry cylinder liners. Mechanical fuel injection metered the fuel, and the engine produced 170 brake horsepower. This engine was powerful enough to propel these cars to a top speed between 115 to 125 miles per hour.

Replacing the 2.2-liter six, the 250SE's 2.5-liter engine had a longer stroke, seven main bearings, mechanical fuel injection, and 30 additional horses. While it offered more power and torque over the smaller engine, it was less fuel efficient and, as noted above, there were some problems with this version of the inline six.

Both the 2.5- and 3.0-liter cars were replaced in early 1968 with the introduction of cars powered by an all-new 2.8-liter SOHC six. This improved design engine cranked out 180 SAE horsepower and was smooth running and powerful enough to move the car along briskly. As good as this engine was, more was coming soon.

In late 1969, a new V-8 was introduced, and the W111 coupe and convertibles were the first models to receive the new engine. A 90-degree eight-cylinder with an SOHC in each bank, Mercedes was planning for the future. With Bosch

D-jetronic fuel injection, transistorized ignition, 9.5:1 compression delivering more than 1 horsepower per cubic inch—230 brake horsepower from 213.5 cubic inches—this engine was the basis for engines that grew to 5.6 liters. A four-speed manual transmission or four-speed automatic backed these engines. A five-speed manual was available as an option from late 1969 on. A fair number of cars were equipped with the automatic, which perhaps was not surprising, thanks to their luxurious nature.

The suspension was cloned from the W111 sedans and had a few minor changes. A slightly lower ride height and beefier springs compensated for the additional weight of the coupe and convertible. In late 1965, a stronger rear axle from the W108 S-class sedans and larger disc brakes were added. The larger brakes meant the cars used 14-inch wheels.

The 220SE was equipped with front discs and rear drums, which actually made it the first Mercedes-Benz production car to have them since it came to market just prior to the 300SL's release, which had disc brakes all around. By late 1963, the 300SE and 250SE models were upgraded to a dual-circuit hydraulic assisted four-wheel disc system. The later 280SE and the 280SE 3.5 continued with power-assisted four-wheel discs.

The interiors of the coupes and convertibles were plush and well appointed for their time. A leather-covered dash with wood accents, deep carpeting, and leather seating were normal, although cloth was also available. Rear seating could be either a rear bench or individual seats. The round speedometer and tachometer flanked a vertical stack of gauges for water temp, fuel, oil, and electrical charging. A Becker Grand Prix radio was located in the center of the dash. Air conditioning could also be fitted and was mounted between the center console and the lower dash.

The convertible top is manually operated and thickly padded with six layers of cloth, insulation, padding, and a full headliner to conceal the steel framework. Each top took two eight-hour days to complete. A leather boot for a clean and finished appearance covers the folded top. Make sure the boot is available at the purchase.

Options for these cars included power-assisted steering, automatic transmission, individual rear seats, ivory-colored steering wheel and matching shift knob, seatbelts, whitewall and radial tires, electric windows, central locking, headrests, and six-piece fitted luggage, which is a very rare find. Sunroofs could be specified for the coupes. The optional column-mounted shifter also included a center armrest that could be folded down to offer seating for three in the front seat.

Overall, rust is the major enemy. Age is another enemy, thanks to previous owner neglect and improper or inadequate repairs. Parts are getting harder to locate, and small trim items are costly to replace.

Typically, the convertibles retain a higher value than coupes. The W112 300SE is probably the more rare of this model. These cars were head-turners when new, and they still draw a crowd. Parts are still generally available and restoring one can be done; however, expect it to be expensive.

These coupes and convertibles are beautiful cars, and when properly restored they still bring good money. Expect to find some euro-spec cars in this group. They are generally okay as long as rust-related issues have been addressed. Also watch for the occasional conversion of a coupe to convertible by checking the number plate on the radiator core support for the chassis type, but know the number plates are riveted on and could be changed.

The 220SEb is the earliest version of the W111 and has minor differences. The external rearview mirror is located on the left front fender. The grille on this 1961 model is taller and more narrow than the cars from 1970 and on.

Make sure that the chassis plate is in place, because it contains important information about the car. The third line shows this is a 111.025 chassis type, which is correct for a 280SE Cabriolet with the 2.8-liter engine.

This particular 280SE was a special order with option deletions. There is no air conditioning or radio. The black steering wheel and shift knob replaced the white wheel and knob in 1970.

Check the VIN plate in the driver's doorjamb. The first six positions of the VIN should match the chassis plate in the engine compartment. If not, be suspicious. If both are missing, be very suspicious.

With a Bosch D-Jetronic fuel-injection and transistorized ignition, the 3.5-liter V-8 produces 230 brake horsepower at 6,500 rpm, which is more than enough to move the 3,600-pound coupe. Look for fluid leaks, and have the engine and transmission checked by a knowledgeable mechanic.

Confirm that the chassis plate is in place, because it contains important information about the car. The third line shows this is a 111.026 chassis type, which is correct for a 280SE 3.5 Coupe.

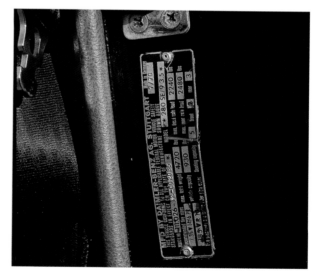

The VIN plate in the driver's doorjamb tells the month and year the car was built, the chassis type (111.026), VIN, and other information.

Common Parts List: W111 220SEb Coupe and Convertible, 1960–1965

Engine:
Oil filter	$4.60
Fuel filter	$7.75
Fuel pump(s)	$645.00
Starter	$177.00 (rebuilt)
Alternator	$113.50 (rebuilt)
Water pump	$199.00

Body:
Headlight	$6.00
Taillight lens	$137.00

Exhaust:
Center muffler	$232.00
Rear muffler	$264.00

Chassis:
Brake master	$248.00
Front rotor	$132.00 each
14. Front pads (set)	$81.00
15. Front shocks	$145.00 each
16. Rear shocks	$145.00 each

Technical Specifications: W111 220SEb, 1960–1965

Engine:
Type	SOHC inline six
Displacement cc/ci	2,195/133.9
Compression ratio	8.7:1
Bhp @ rpm	134 @ 5,000
Torque ft-lb @ rpm	152 @ 4,100
Fuel injection	Bosch mechanical fuel injection
Fuel requirement	Unleaded

Chassis/drivetrain:
Transmission	Four-speed manual, optional four-speed automatic
Steering	Recirculating ball, servo assisted
Front suspension	Independent, coil springs, tube shocks, anti-roll bar
Rear suspension	Single joint, coil springs, tube shocks, anti-roll bar
Differential	4.10:1

General:
Wheelbase	108.3
Weight	3,435
Wheels	Steel, 13x6.0
Tires	13x6.70
Brake system	Front disc/rear drum
0–60 mph	13.3 sec
Maximum speed mph	106
Fuel economy:	city/hwy
EPA estimated mpg	17/23

Common Parts List: W111 250SE Coupe and Convertible, 1966–1967

Engine:

Oil filter	$4.60
Fuel filter	$7.75
Fuel pump(s)	$645.00 (electric)
Starter	$177.00 (rebuilt)
Alternator	$113.50 (rebuilt)
Fan clutch	$238.00
Water pump	$161.00

Body:

Headlight	$6.00

Exhaust:

Center muffler	$232.00
Rear muffler	$264.00

Chassis:

Brake master	$266.00
Front rotor	$93.00 each
Front pads (set)	$30.00
Front shocks	$145.00 each
Rear shocks	$145.00 each

Common Parts List: W112 300SE Coupe and Convertible, 1961–1967

Engine:

Oil filter	$4.60
Fuel filter	$7.75
Fuel pump(s)	$645.00 (electric)
Starter	$177.00 (rebuilt)
Alternator	$113.50 (rebuilt)
Fan clutch	$238.00
Water pump	$161.00

Body:

Headlight assembly	$6.00
Taillight lens	$137.00

Exhaust:

Center muffler	$232.00
Rear muffler	$264.00

Chassis:

Brake master	$266.00
Front rotor	$132.00 each
Front pads (set)	$81.00
Front shocks	$145.00 each
Rear shocks	$158.00 each

Rating Chart: W111/112 Coupes and Cabrios, 1960–1972

Model	Comfort/Amenities	Reliability	Collectibility	Parts/Service Availability	Est. Annual Repair Costs
220SEb Coupe	★★★	★★	★★★★	★★	★★★½
220SEb Conv.	★★★½	★★	★★★★½	★★	★★★½
300SE Coupe	★★★	★★★½	★★★★	★★★½	★★★½
300SE Conv.	★★★	★★★½	★★★★½	★★★½	★★★½
250SE Coupe	★★★	★★★½	★★★★	★★★½	★★★½
250SE Conv.	★★★	★★★½	★★★★½	★★★½	★★★½
280SE Coupe	★★★★½	★★★	★★★★	★★★	★★★½
280SE Conv.	★★★★½	★★★	★★★★½	★★★	★★★½
280SE Coupe	★★★★½	★★★	★★★★	★★★	★★★½
280SE Conv.	★★★★½	★★★	★★★★½	★★★	★★★½

Technical Specifications: W111 250SE Coupe and Convertible, 1965–1967

Engine:

Type	SOHC inline six
Displacement cc/ci	2,496/152.3
Compression ratio	9.3:1
Bhp @ rpm	150 @ 5,500
Torque ft-lb @ rpm	159 @ 4,200
Fuel injection	Bosch mechanical fuel injection
Fuel requirement	Unleaded

Chassis/drivetrain:

Transmission	Four-speed manual, optional four-speed automatic
Steering	Recirculating ball, servo assisted
Front suspension	Independent, coil springs, tube shocks, anti-roll bar
Rear suspension	Single joint, coil springs, tube shocks, anti-roll bar
Differential	3.92:1

General:

Wheelbase	108.3
Weight	3,435
Wheels	Steel, 14x6.0
Tires	13x6.70
Brake system	Front disc/rear drum
0–60 mph	13.3 sec
Maximum speed mph	106
Fuel economy:	city/hwy
EPA estimated mpg	17/23

Technical Specifications: W112 300SE Coupe and Convertible, 1961–1965

Engine:

Type	SOHC, inline six
Displacement cc/ci	2,996/182.8
Compression ratio	8.7:1
Bhp @ rpm (DIN)	170 @ 5,400
Torque ft-lb @ rpm	183 @ 4,000
Injection type	Bosch electronic
Fuel requirement	Leaded

Chassis/drivetrain:

Transmission	Four-speed manual
Steering	Recirculating ball, power-assisted
Front suspension	Independent, coil springs, tube shocks
Rear suspension	Single-joint swing axle, coil springs, tube shocks, anti-roll bar
Differential	3.69:1 or 3.92:1

General:

Wheelbase	108.3
Weight	3,649
Wheels	Steel, 14x6
Tires	185 H 14
Brake system	Four-wheel disc
0–60 mph	12 sec (est.)
Maximum speed mph	115–120 mph (est.)
Fuel economy:	
EPA estimated mpg	15–17 mpg

Common Parts List: W111 280SE Coupe and Convertible, 1968–1972

Engine:

Oil filter	$4.60
Fuel filter	$7.75
Fuel pump(s)	$645.00 (electric)
Starter	$177.00 (rebuilt)
Alternator	$137.00 (rebuilt)
Fan clutch	$238.00
Water pump	$161.00

Body:

Headlight assembly	$6.00
Taillight lens	$137.00

Exhaust:

Center muffler	$232.00
Rear muffler	$264.00

Chassis:

Brake master	$248.00
Front rotor	$130.00 each
Front pads (set)	$30.00
Front shocks	$145.00 each
Rear shocks	$145.00 each

Technical specifications: W111 280SE Coupe and Convertible, 1968–1972

Engine:

Type	SOHC inline six
Displacement cc/ci	2778/169.5
Compression ratio	9.5:1
Bhp @ rpm	180 (SAE) @ 5,750
Torque ft-lb @ rpm	193.2 @ 4,500
Injection type	Bosch six-plunger pump
Fuel requirement	Leaded

Chassis/drivetrain:

Transmission	Four-speed manual or automatic
Steering	Recirculating ball, servo assisted
Front suspension	Independent, coil springs, tube shocks, anti-roll bar
Rear suspension	single joint, coil springs, tube shocks, anti-roll bar
Differential	4.08:1 (U.S.)

General:

Wheelbase	108.3	
Weight:		
Coupe	3,330	
Convertible	3,495	
Wheels	Steel, 14x7	
Tires	185 H 14	
Brake system:	Four-wheel disc, power-assisted	
Front	10.8-inch discs	
Rear	11.0-inch discs	
0–60 mph	10.5 sec	
Maximum speed mph:		
Manual	118 (est.)	
Automatic	115 (est.)	
Fuel capacity	U.S. gallons	21.7
Fuel economy:		
EPA estimated mpg	18.75 mpg	

Common Parts List: W111 280SE 3.5 Coupe and Convertible, 1969–1972

Engine:

Oil filter	$8.00
Fuel filter	$33.50
Fuel pump(s)	$625.00 (electric)
Starter	$177.00 (rebuilt)
Alternator	$136.00 (rebuilt)
Fan clutch	$238.00
Water pump	$155.50

Body:

Headlight assembly	$6.00
Taillight lens	$137.00

Exhaust:

Center muffler	$232.00
Rear muffler	$264.00

Chassis:

Brake master	$248.00
Front rotor	$130.00 each
Front pads (set)	$30.00
Front shocks	$145.00 each
Rear shocks	$145.00 each

Technical Specifications: W111 280SE 3.5 Coupe and Convertible, 1969–1971

Engine:

Type	SOHC 90-degree V-8, cast-iron block/aluminum heads
Displacement cc/ci	3,499/213.5
Compression ratio	9.5:1
Bhp @ rpm	230 @ 6,500
Torque ft-lb @ rpm	231 @ 4,200
Injection type	Bosch electronic
Fuel requirement	Leaded

Chassis/drivetrain:

Transmission	Four-speed manual
Steering	Recirculating ball, power-assisted
Front suspension	Independent, coil springs, tube shocks
Rear suspension	Single joint swing axle, coil springs, tube shocks, anti-roll bar
Differential	3.69:1

General:

Wheelbase	108.3
Weight:	
Coupe	3,641 pounds
Convertible	3,463 pounds
Wheels	Steel
Tires	185 H 14
Brake system:	Four-wheel disc
Front	10.8-inch solid discs
Rear	11.0-inch solid discs
0–60 mph	9.5 sec (est.)
Maximum speed mph	127 mph (est.)
Fuel capacity	U.S. gallons 21.7
Fuel economy:	
EPA estimated mpg	15 to 17 mpg

Conversions—Check for coupes that have been converted to convertibles. Verify the last three digits of the chassis (W111.024 or 111.025, etc.); however, this is still not an absolute guarantee.

Rust—The W111 and W112 cars have a history of rusting. Check the fenders, doors, rear license plate area, and floorboards. Replacement panels are available; however, repairs will be costly.

Body damage—Along with rust, check for accident damage or repairs to the nose and tail.

Engines—The 2.5-liter is prone to problems with rod and main bearings. Today's technology can address this, but the cost of a complete rebuild can be high. The 3.0-liter is an all-alloy engine. Use of incorrect coolant can lead to corrosion in the water passages and result in overheating. Repairs can be expensive, and parts are getting harder to find.

Steering wheels and shift knobs—Beginning with the 1970 models, a black steering wheel and shift knob were standard, and white was optional.

Air suspension—The air suspension systems on the 300E have been troublesome and are expensive to repair. The parts are difficult to locate and are expensive.

Missing pieces—Find as complete a car as you can. The lower the miles, the better. Some body and trim pieces are NLA, and not all parts will interchange with the sedans.

COSTA MESA
CALIFORNIA
ROENTGN
BRUCE STRAUSS AUTOCARE

Chapter 6

W114 250C/280C: 1969–1976
Basic History

The 250C coupe was introduced late summer 1969 and overlapped the larger W111 chassis 280SE. The 250C shared its design and mechanicals with the W114 sedans. Except for the longer doors and quarter panels, the W114 coupes and sedans are visually the same up to the tops of the fenders.

The greenhouse of the coupe bears some resemblance to the Pagoda roof of the W113 SLs to the point of having two chrome strips that double as attaching points for roof racks and rain guttering. The roofline of the coupe is 2 inches lower than its sedan sibling, and like the 280SE coupes, the W114 is a pillarless design that leaves a clean, airy look when the side windows are rolled down.

Designed and introduced before the 5-mile-per-hour bumper and emissions requirements of the early 1970s were put in place, the Mercedes-Benz coupes, like other manufacturers' designs of the same era, were retrofitted with larger bumpers that were not flattering.

Emissions requirements of the early 1970s were a challenge. The engines of this period tended to have a variety of smog-related accessories attached to them and did not always run and perform as well as preemissions engines.

The 250C used a single-cam 2,778-cc version of the older 2.5-liter engine, either with dual carbs (250C) or Bosch D-Jetronic (in the 250CE model). The extra 300 cc, in some respects, were a concession to more stringent U.S. emissions requirements and their detrimental effect to the 2.5-liter's power output.

These emissions control–era engines were tuned to run lean, and as a result, the carbureted cars don't run as well as the fuel-injected cars. Engines from this time also tend to run hotter (a side effect of emissions control engines being leaned out), which can lead to overheating, especially if the cooling system has not been properly maintained.

With the 1972 emissions requirements making things even tougher, Mercedes-Benz was fast at work developing a new 2.8-liter engine. Displacing 2,746 cc, this new engine was a DOHC, seven main-bearing inline six. Featuring a crossflow head, single duplex chain, and the same rocker arms as used in the 4.5-liter V-8s, the U.S.-spec engines used a single Solex carburetor and developed 120 brake horsepower. Non-U.S. market engines had Bosch D-Jetronic fuel injection and made nearly 160 brake horsepower.

A four-speed manual transmission was standard, and a four-speed, fluid-coupled automatic was optional. By 1973, Mercedes followed most other manufacturers and switched to a four-speed automatic with a torque converter. Shifting and performance of the new automatic were greatly improved.

Also carried on the option list was a five-speed manual transmission. Do not expect to see many W114 coupes with this transmission. Dealers in the United States did not exactly encourage ordering this transmission.

The suspension was brought over from the sedan and was independent front and rear with unequal-length A-arms, coil springs, tube shocks, and anti-roll bar in the front. At the rear, semi-trailing arms, coil springs, tube shocks, and anti-roll bars were standard with automatic leveling optional. Brakes were power-assisted four-wheel discs, and radial tires were available.

In the interior, the seats are mounted lower, a result of the 2-inch-lower roofline. Rear seats are also a bit farther forward than the sedans to accommodate the rake of the rear window. Trunk space is 17.5 cubic feet, which is 1.5 cubic feet larger than the sedan.

Instruments include a large round speedometer and tachometer. In the center of the cluster are a gas gauge, warning lights, and turn-signal indicators. Although not initially available, a wood veneer inlay (which was advertised at the time as safer because it would not splinter in an accident) dressed up the dashboard. The radio and air-conditioning controls are located in the center console. The A/C is better integrated in these cars; although typical for the time, it is not the equal of comparable American cars.

Remembering the era when these cars were available, the color combinations tended to be conservative. Two-tone paint schemes with the top painted a different color from the body were popular. Metallic paint, the popular two-stage paint that is prone to fading and difficult to match, was an extracost option.

A signal-seeking AM/FM radio with electric antenna, air conditioning, power steering, a sunroof, electric window lifts, a heated rear window, tinted glass, vinyl upholstery, radial tires, rear speaker, and front center armrest were available options. Alloy wheels and an optional five-speed gearbox could be selected from the option list.

The option list was extensive and, at the time, it seemed like everything you wanted was optional (and buyers paid for each of them).

Production of the 250C ended in midsummer 1976. The 280C ceased production later that summer. With approximately 11,800 250Cs built between 1969 and 1976 and slightly more than 13,100 of the 2.8-liter DOHC coupes made during its five-year run, these are relatively low-volume cars.

The W114 coupes are a conservative design based on solid underpinnings and are often overlooked. The pre-1974 cars feature the better-looking bumpers (pre-5-mile-per-hour bumpers) and have slightly more power than the later DOHC-powered cars. The later model cars do have the smoother DOHC six and may be better equipped. Rust can be an issue, but mechanicals are shared with the sedans, and plenty of spare parts are available.

While the W114 coupes are probably not as desirable as the classic W111 coupes, they can be a nice, reliable daily driver that offers traditional Mercedes-Benz reliability.

Pre-1974 models have smaller bumpers and taillights. Look for damage from rear-end collisions and rust from repairs. The two small Mercedes emblems on the left are not original and probably would replace the "automatic" script that was there originally.

This 1970 250C is dirty and dusty, but almost everything is there. The piece of wood wedged along the right side of the radiator and electronic ignition is not original, but the A/C is. The VIN plate is missing from the radiator support.

The aluminum VIN sticker is attached to the driver-side A-pillar on U.S. market cars. If it is not there, it may be a gray market model. The number should match the VIN located in the driver's doorjamb and the one stamped on the right frame rail in the engine bay.

The leather in this car is in pretty good condition. Remove the rubber floor mats and lift the carpeting to look for rust in the floorboards. The dash has a crack right above the glove-box door. This radio is not the original, but ask the owners if they still have the original radio.

The trunk space is generous. Be sure to pull the mat and check for rust in the trunk floor, corners, wheelwells, and shock towers. Remove the spare to check the condition of the spare tire well. The jack and tool roll may be missing, and replacements will be hard to locate.

In addition to the larger 5-mile-per-hour bumpers, the taillight lenses have been redesigned to incorporate the self-cleaning ribs on Mercedes from this era. Look for rust in the lower corners and license plate areas.

The instrumentation is large and easy to read. There is a reminder to use unleaded fuel in the center of the cluster. The Becker radio is the original unit. Air conditioning was factory installed and works surprisingly well for a car from this era. The wood inlays in the dash have held up well. Not all cars will be this nice.

DOT safety requirements resulted in better seatbelt designs compared to the earlier cars. A third, center seatbelt is available and three can occupy the rear seat. The center armrest pulls out and swivels down. Headroom is adequate, but it is somewhat more limited than in sedan versions.

The trunk is generous and offers plenty of room for luggage. Remove the rubber mat and look all around for evidence of rust or crash repairs.

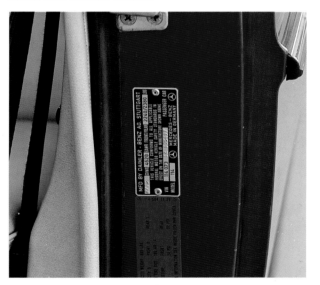

This is a close-up look at the driver-side doorjamb manufacturer's plate. Look for evidence of overspray to indicate a repaint or damage repairs. Even though this car has been resprayed, the job was done well because there is no overspray and the color matches perfectly. Information on the VIN plate tells us that this car was built in February 1975.

Common Parts List: W114 250C, 1969–1976

Engine:

Oil filter	$4.60
Fuel filter	$13.00
Fuel pump(s)	$274.00
Starter	$177.00 (rebuilt)
Alternator	$113.50 (rebuilt)
Fan clutch	$238.00
Water pump	$161.00

Body:

Headlight frame	$330.00

Exhaust:

Center muffler	$170.00
Rear muffler	$298.00

Chassis:

Brake master	$248.00
Front rotor	$93.00 each
Front pads (set)	$30.00
Front shocks	$139.00 each
Rear shocks	$145.00 each

Common Parts List: W114–280C, 1972–1976

Engine:

Oil filter	$8.00
Fuel filter	$13.00
Fuel pump(s)	$185.00
Starter	$177.00 (rebuilt)
Alternator	$167.00 (rebuilt)
Fan clutch	$238.00
Water pump	$161.00

Body:

Headlight frame	$330.00
Taillight lens	$96.00

Exhaust:

Center muffler	$170.00
Rear muffler	$298.00

Chassis:

Brake master	$350.00
Front rotor	$40.50 each
Front pads (set)	$48.00
Front shocks	$139.00 each
Rear shocks	$145.00 each

Rating Chart
W114 250C/280C Coupes, 1969–1976

Model	Comfort/Amenities	Reliability	Collectibility	Parts/Service	Est. Annual Service Cost
250C	★★↓	★★↓	★★★↓	★★↓	★★★↓
280C	★★↓	★★★	★★★↓	★★★	★★★↓

Technical Specifications: W114 250C, 1969–1976

Engine:

Type	DOHC, inline six
Displacement cc/ci	2778/169.5
Compression ratio	8.7:1
Bhp @ rpm	157 @ 5,400
Torque ft-lb @ rpm	181 @ 3,800
Induction:	
250C	Two dual downdraft Zenith 35/40 INAT
250CE	Bosch electronic
Fuel requirement:	Premium, leaded

Chassis/drivetrain:

Transmission	Four-speed manual, optional four-speed automatic
Steering	Recirculating ball, servo assisted
Front suspension	Unequal-length A-arms, coil springs, tube shocks, anti-roll bar
Rear suspension	Semi-trailing arms, coil springs, hydropnuematic leveling struts, anti-roll bar
Differential	3.92:1

General:

Wheelbase	108.3
Weight	3,800
Wheels	14x5? J
Tires	175HR-14
Brake system:	Four-wheel disc, power-assisted
Front	10.2-inch discs
Rear	10.7-inch discs
0–60 mph	13.6 sec
Maximum speed mph	115 (est.)
Fuel economy:	
EPA estimated mpg	16

Technical Specifications: W114 280C, 1971–1976

Engine:

Type	DOHC, inline six
Displacement cc/ci	2,746/168
Compression ratio	8.0:1
Bhp @ rpm	120 (SAE) @ 4,800
Torque ft-lb @ rpm	143 @ 2,800
Induction	Dual downdraft Soles 4A1
Fuel requirement	Premium, unleaded

Chassis/drivetrain:

Transmission	Four-speed manual, optional four-speed automatic
Steering	Recirculating ball, servo assisted
Front suspension	Unequal-length A-arms, coil springs, tube shocks, anti-roll bar
Rear suspension	Semi-trailing arms, coil springs, hydropnuematic leveling struts, anti-roll bar
Differential	3.69:1

General:

Wheelbase	108.3
Weight	3,200
Wheels	14x6 J
Tires	185HR-14
Brake system:	Four-wheel disc, power-assisted
Front	10.8-inch discs
Rear	11.0-inch discs
0–60 mph	13.0 sec (est.)
Maximum Speed mph	118 (est.)
Fuel economy:	city/hwy
EPA estimated mpg	16/18

Cooling system—Check the overall condition of the cooling system. German car cooling systems of this era are marginal in warmer climates. Check radiator and heater hoses for soft spots, bulges, and the like.

Carburetors—The original-equipment carbs have a history of the bases warping and causing vacuum leaks. Avoid the temptation to tighten when the engine is hot, which makes the condition worse.

A/C system—Many had A/C installed at the time of delivery. Check that it works and look at the installation in the engine compartment. Have the mounting brackets checked for any problems such as cracks.

European cars—Buyers may find European cars available. They are old enough that they may be exempt from local smog requirements. Be sure to confirm that all the paperwork is in order and the car can be registered.

Rust—Look in the usual places for rust, including the fenders, doors, floorboards, and where trim attaches to bodies. Lift carpets and mats in the passenger compartment and trunk.

Chapter 7

W123 280CE/ 300CD: 1978–1985

Basic History

First shown to the public at the 1977 Geneva show, the W123-chassis 280CE coupe followed the introduction of the sedans by about one year. While design of the W123 had originally begun in 1970, these coupes made their appearance in the United States in early 1978.

Built on a wheelbase that is 4 inches shorter than the sedan, these coupes made more of a statement about image and luxury than they did about performance. Rear-seat legroom and headroom are tighter as a result of the lowered roofline, and the shortened wheelbase tends to have a choppier ride. Except for the shorter wheelbase, the coupes use exactly the same mechanicals as the sedans and estate wagons.

The passenger cell is stronger and incorporates front and rear crumple zones that are engineered to collapse in a predetermined manner, which stemmed from lessons learned through crash testing. The passenger compartment is further protected by side-impact beams and roof supports that are narrower for better visibility and stronger in the event of a rollover.

The steering column collapses and deflects away from the driver, and the steering wheel has an energy-absorbing center hub. Front seatbelt attaching points were relocated to the seat frames to provide better positioning of the shoulder and lap belt combination during accident impacts. The spare tire is mounted under the trunk floorboards and serves as additional protection during rear impacts.

Zero-offset steering geometry, wider track, and anti-dive front suspension contributed to greater driver control during emergency maneuvers. The mandatory 5-mile-per-hour U.S. bumpers are better integrated in these cars, although compared to today's cars, they still look like add-ons.

One of the objectives of the new design was to make servicing and repairs easier, which showed that Mercedes was thinking about reducing the long-term costs of maintenance. The engine hood latch design allows the hood to be opened to a nearly vertical position, a feature that continues to this day. Extensive rust proofing was employed and included zinc-coating the entire body and applying rust-preventative coatings under the car and inside the hollow body cavities.

The traditional Mercedes-Benz independent front suspension featured double A-arms, tube shocks with coil springs, and an anti-roll bar. Rear suspension used semi-trailing arms, coil springs, tube shocks, and an anti-roll bar.

The brake system is common across all the W123 chassis, which saved production costs because there are fewer parts to inventory, and it made repairs easier. The power-assisted four-wheel discs used dual brake circuits as backup in case one system failed.

Engine choices included the 2.8-liter DOHC inline six or a five-cylinder diesel—a first for any of the luxury two-door coupes. The gas-powered coupes were available from early 1978 through 1985. The diesel-powered cars were built exclusively for the North American market and were not available in other markets. Between September 1977 and August 1981, the diesel was not turbocharged. Introduced in September 1981, the turbocharged diesel continued until production of the W123 coupes ended in August 1985. The only transmission available in the United States was a four-speed automatic.

A minor facelift for the exterior happened in 1983. The air intake grilles in front of the windshield were blacked out and the moldings for the windshield pillars were redesigned.

The 1985 300CD turbodiesel models received a trap oxidizer to meet the more stringent California emissions standards. There were problems with this device and

Mercedes-Benz offered to replace the part in 1996 with an improved oxidation catalyst design, often at no cost to the owner. Ask for records or proof that the part was fixed and have this checked before completing a purchase. Expect this to be an expensive fix, but you may be able to work with your local dealer to install the 1997 catalyst system updates.

The dash cluster is made up of three circular instruments. A large speedometer marked in both mph and kmph was flanked on the left by a combination fuel, oil, and temperature gauge, and on the right was a combination tachometer and analog clock. Burled walnut inlays separate the upper and lower dash with eyeball vents at both ends and two circular vents in the middle. The center console has more burled walnut, the HVAC controls, radio, shift quadrant, and electric window buttons.

The individual front bucket seats are generous and comfortable, and a center armrest was attached to the driver's seat. The outboard seatbelt anchor point is over the shoulder of the front seat passengers. The front seat backs fold forward for access to the rear passenger area. In the rear, a dropdown center armrest allows seating for three, but it is cozy. Outboard rear passengers have three-point seatbelts that come over shoulder and attach in the middle. The third passenger makes do with a lap belt that can be stowed between the upper and lower seat cushions.

Options included a manual or electric sunroof, metallic paint, and alloy wheels. Basically, these vehicles were equipped with all the amenities one would expect of a luxury coupe.

Rust can be an issue for these cars. Although factory rust proofing was improved with these coupes, look for evidence in the usual places. Presence of rust can often be an indication of damage repairs. Authorized Mercedes-Benz repair facilities will properly rustproof repair work, but others might not.

Verify that the vacuum-operated systems, such as the central locking, function correctly. Malfunctions in the system can manifest in a variety of manners, such as harsh shifting (the diesel cars have a vacuum pump that supplies vacuum for shifting the transmission and operating the central locking system). If the diesel engine continues to run after the ignition is turned off, try locking the doors and then turn off the engine. These types of problems can be indications of vacuum leaks.

Maintenance records are especially important for the diesel-powered cars. It is important to know that oil changes have been done regularly. Also, the climate control system should be checked thoroughly for operation.

While gas-powered coupes are not high on the collector's list of cars, they are fewer in number than diesels. Performance of the diesels is expectedly slow. Reliability and longevity of the diesel engines is renowned and the 300CD coupes will literally run forever. The W123 coupes still look good today and make exceptionally good daily drivers.

Verify the presence of the manufacturer's VIN plate and stickers in the driver's doorjamb. The VIN should match with the one on the A-pillar. Missing or painted-over stickers could be an indication of accident repair.

Check the air cleaner mountings for deterioration. Age and exposure to diesel fuel can cause them to collapse and disintegrate. The battery needs to be in top shape because diesel engines take more cranking power to start.

The large and easy-to-spot taillights are ribbed to help keep dirt off the lenses. Look for evidence of accident damage and original paint. Engine maintenance records are important on diesel-powered cars, so examine them to verify regular oil changes.

Common Parts List: W123 280CE, 1979–1981

Engine:

Oil filter	$8.00
Fuel filter	$45.00
Fuel pump(s)	$266.00
Starter	$177.00 (rebuilt)
Alternator	$193.00 (rebuilt)
Radiator	$288.00
Fan clutch	$238.00
Water pump	$89.00

Body:

Front bumper:	
Bumper end	$78.00
Bumper impact strip	$114.00
Headlight assembly	$378.00
Taillight lens	$184.00

Exhaust:

Rear muffler	$139.00

Chassis:

Brake master	$350.00
Front rotor	$40.50 each
Front pads (set)	$48.00
Front shocks:	
Standard	$85.00 each
Heavy duty	$116.00 each
Rear shocks	$132.00 each

Common Parts List: W123–300CD & Turbo, 1978–1985

Engine:

Oil filter	$13.50
Fuel filter:	$11.00
Pre-filter	$2.00
Fuel Pump:	
Non-turbo	$220.00
Turbodiesel	$214.00
Starter	$227.75 (rebuilt)
Alternator:	
Non-turbo	$167.00 (rebuilt)
Turbodiesel	$193.00 (rebuilt)
Radiator:	
Non-turbo	$346.00
Turbodiesel	$520.00
Fan Clutch	$238.00
Water pump	$89.00

Body:

Front bumper:	
Bumper end	$78.00
Bumper impact strip	$114.00

Rear Bumper:	
Bumper end	$74.00
Bumper impact strip	$98.00
Headlight assembly	$378.00
Taillight lens	$184.00

Exhaust:

Rear muffler:	
Non-turbo	$149.00
Turbodiesel	$104.00

Chassis:

Brake Master:	
Non-turbo	$350.00
Turbodiesel	$322.00
Front rotor	$40.50 each
Front Pads(set)	$48.00
Front shocks:	
Standard	$85.00 each
Heavy duty	$116.00 each
Rear shocks	$132.00 each

Technical Specifications: W123 280CE, 1978–1985

Engine:

Type	DOHC, inline six
Displacement cc/ci	2,746/168
Compression ratio	8.0:1
Bhp @ rpm	123 @ 5,000
Torque ft-lb @ rpm	143 @ 3,600
Injection type	Bosch
Fuel Requirement	Premium unleaded

Chassis/drivetrain:

Steering	Recirculating ball, servo assisted
Front suspension	Unequal-length A-arms, coil springs, tube shocks, anti-roll bar
Rear suspension	Semi-trailing arms, coil springs, tube shocks, anti-roll bar
Differential	3.54:1

General:

Wheelbase	106.7
Weight	3,510
Wheels	14x6J
Tires	195/70HR-14
Brake system:	Four-wheel disc, power-assisted
Front	10.9 inch solid discs
Rear	11.0 inch solid discs
0–60 mph	10.8 sec
Maximum Speed mph	124 (est.)
Fuel economy:	city/hwy
EPA estimated mpg	18/21

Technical Specifications:
W123 300CD, 1978–1985

Engine:

Type:

5/77–9/81	Five-cylinder, inline diesel
9/81–8/85	Five-cylinder, inline diesel, turbo-charged

Displacement cc/ci:

5/77 – 9/81	3,005/183.4
9/81 – 8/85	2,998/182.9

Compression ratio:

5/77–9/81	21.0:1
9/81–8/85	21.5:1

Bhp @ rpm:

5/77–9/81	77 @ 4,000
9/81–8/85	118 @ 4,350

Torque ft-lb @ rpm:

5/77–9/81	115 @ 2,400
9/81–8/85	177 @ 2,400
Injection type	Bosch injection
Fuel requirement	Diesel

Chassis/drivetrain:

Transmission	Four-speed automatic
Steering	Recirculating ball, power-assisted
Front suspension	Double A-arms, coil springs, tube shocks, anti-roll bar.
Rear suspension	Semi-trailing arms, coil springs, tube shocks, anti-roll bar
Differential	3.46:1

General:

Wheelbase	106.7
Weight	3,495
Wheels	14x6J
Tires	195/70HR-14
Brake system:	Four-wheel disc, power-assisted
Front	10.9 inch solid discs
Rear	11.0 inch solid discs
0–60 mph	21.7 sec
Maximum speed mph	92 (est.)
Fuel economy:	city/hwy
EPA estimated mpg	23/28

Rating Chart
W123 280CE/300CD Coupes 1978–1985

Model	Comfort/Amenities	Reliability	Collectibility	Parts/Service	Est. Annual Repair Costs
280CE	★★★	★★★★⯪	★★⯪	★★★★⯪	★★★
300CD	★★★	★★★★	★★⯪	★★★★⯪	★★★
300CD Turbo	★★★	★★★★	★★⯪	★★★★⯪	★★★

Air intake—Look for damage below the front bumper from bumping into curbs or parking lot stops. This could result in blocking the airflow to the radiator and engine air intakes.

Trap oxidizers—If you live in California, be sure to have the car checked to see if the trap oxidizer has been replaced with the updated part.

Plastic tank radiators—Watch for telltale white residue around seams and hose necks to identify leaks. Try to confirm if the newer style Behr radiator is installed. Its reinforced hose necks reduce the tendency to crack/fail.

Electrical accessories—Check to make sure the mirrors, seat adjusters, windows, sunroof, radio, and antenna work.

Diesels and vacuum-operated systems—Check the function of the vacuum-operated seat back locks and central locking systems. Diesels do not create their own vacuum and have a belt-driven vacuum pump. Over time the various vacuum lines can crack, which lead to malfunctions with the central locking system.

Various noises—Listen for any noises from the differential. Brake squeal could indicate incorrect pads.

Leaking power steering—The power steering system should not leak. It could be a power steering pump seal or lines.

Trunk seals—Defective trunk seals can let water into the trunk. Check under the floor covering, the outboard corners, and in the spare tire well.

Door seals—To diagnose leaky door seals, lift the carpeting where you can and feel for any dampness and look underneath for signs of rusting.

Rust—Look in the lower sills, around the wheel arches, and the bottoms of the doors. The drain holes plug up and the moisture gets trapped inside the doors.

Automatic transmissions—Check that the automatic transmission shifts smoothly. Clunking and hard shifts can indicate troubles, as well as excessive slipping when gear changes take place. These problems could also indicate troubles with the vacuum system.

Alloy wheels—Check alloy wheels for signs of damage, such as curb scrapes and pothole damage on the inner edges.

Chapter 8

W203 C230 Kompressor/C320 Sport Coupe: 2002 on
Basic History

Intended to appeal to the more youthful market, the C230 Kompressor Sport Coupe broadened the C-class model range and opened the door to buyers who in the past may not have been able to buy a Mercedes. The C230 seems to have succeeded where BMW's similar concept, the 318ti hatchback, did not. Speaking of a hatchback, Mercedes-Benz prefers to call these models a Sport Coupe.

Although it was 7 inches shorter than the sedan, the general design of the C230K/C320 Sport Coupe resembles the C-class. These vehicles share the 106.9-inch wheelbase, suspension, steering, and brakes with the sedans. In front, there are MacPherson struts with two separate lower links, coil springs, twin-tube gas pressurized shocks, and an anti-roll bar. In the rear is the now familiar MB multilink design (originally seen in the 190 sedan) with updated track links, hub carriers, subframe, and revised elastokinematics. The brakes are four-wheel discs, and the fronts are vented and the rears are solid.

The external mirrors and headlights are shared with the sedans, but no other body panels are shared between them. The bumper surround is distinct and the grille is closer in design to the larger coupes and roadsters because it has horizontal bars and a center-mounted star.

Electronically, the Sport Coupes use fiber optics in place of copper wire and the various systems are interconnected. This allows function switching of exterior lighting, such as if a front turn signal bulb fails, the car's microprocessors can instruct the corner fog light to function as the turn signal until the failed bulb is replaced.

The third brake light uses 20 LEDs that illuminate up to 50 milliseconds quicker than normal light bulbs. This gives drivers behind the Sport Coupe more time to react. Like the larger Mercedes cars, the electronic ignition switch takes one turn of the key to start, unlike other cars where the switch must be held in the start position during start-up. Old habits die hard and many find they hold the switch in the start position longer than necessary.

An option with the C-class Sport Coupes is an all-glass panorama roof. The front section of the roof is 30 percent larger than a normal sunroof, and when opened, the front section slides up and over the rear portion of the panorama roof. There are electrically operated front and rear retractable shades that are hidden in an overhead crossmember that separates the movable portion from the fixed portion.

The rear hatch or door has a polycarbonate see-through panel below the spoiler that increases rearward vision when backing up. The taillights are nicely integrated into the corners of the rear fenders and flank the rear hatch opening. Underneath the car, time spent in the wind tunnel resulted in streamlining panels that smooth the airflow.

Standard equipment included cloth upholstery, eight airbags, ABS, ESP, ASR traction control, Brake Assist (BAS), BabySmart, COMAND, Roadside Assistance, Flexible Service System (FSS), six-speed manual transmission, dual-zone climate control, cruise control, tilt and telescope steering wheel with multifunction controls, a trip computer, and AM/FM/cassette with antitheft protection.

The list of options included leather upholstery, a five-speed electronically controlled automatic transmission with TouchShift, power front seats with integrated steering wheel adjustments, TeleAid, and the novel panorama roof.

The dash differed slightly from the sedans and had a more closely tailored hood over the primary instruments. The instrument cluster had a multifunction display centered in the speedometer that displayed stereo adjustments (radio station, volume), odometer, trip computer, and the optional

Cockpit Management and Data (COMAND) system information. The 160-mile per hour speedometer is a bit optimistic since the estimated maximum speed for the Sport Coupe is 130 miles per hour.

The front seats have an articulated fold-forward feature that allows easy access in and out of the rear seats. The rear seat backs are split 60/40 and can fold forward to lie nearly flat and make a large cargo area with plenty of carrying capacity—10.2 cubic feet with the seats up and 38.1 cubic feet (nearly 8 cubic feet larger than the C-class sedans) with the seats folded. There is a rear compartment cover that is easily removed. The rear seat headroom and legroom is limited, but the front seats offer plenty of room for those over 6 feet tall.

The front passenger seat is equipped with the MB BabySmart technology that recognizes when infant car seats are being used and disables the passenger side airbag.

TeleAid is activated when any of the eight airbags deploys. The TeleAid system automatically notifies a centralized response unit of the vehicle's location with information that can be provided to police and emergency rescue teams.

The 2.3-liter supercharged engine is shared with the SLK230 roadster, although a new fuel injection and intake manifold (also shared with SLK) improved low-end power and helped to reduce the engine noise levels that SLK and Sport Coupe owners noted.

The 3.2-liter V-6 was added for the 2003 model year and is the same unit found in the C-class sedans, the CLK320, and the SLK320.

In summary, the C230 and C320 Sport Coupes are entry-level Mercedes. Buyers should anticipate finding some high mileage cars. Also watch for cars that were leased and the driver had no long-term interest in the car and deferred maintenance, which may need to be corrected.

The supercharged four-cylinder tends to be a bit on the noisy side, but it does have adequate power. The 3,199-cc V-6 will be smoother and quicker. There have been some complaints that the manual shift linkage is notchy and not precise so expect that when you drive various examples.

The C-class has taken a beating from the consumer groups over reliability and build quality issues. Service technicians can address many of these. With all the electrical systems incorporated in these cars, there have been many reports of electrical glitches that occur and mysteriously fix themselves. Exercise all the electrical functions multiple times during a test drive. Watch for any malfunctions. Nuisance items can often be lived with, but faulty systems such as COMAND and Climate Control could be bad news.

Listen for clicking noises from the Climate Control system. It could be the flap stepper motors. If it is coming from outside, it could be the charcoal canister shut-off valve. If you hear a clicking noise with the engine idling, it may be the fuel system purge valve. If the windshield fogs up above the center vent, there is an updated version of the vent that can be installed.

Owners have experienced problems with the remote key intermittently not locking or unlocking the car. There is a newer version of the remote key that will fix the problem, so check with service technicians on this.

Some cars have experienced bolts breaking in the crossmember that goes across the top of the radiator. Take a look at the bolt heads to see if they are loose or look like they have been replaced and ask for this to be checked at the prepurchase inspection.

Manufacturers' stickers are located in the driver's doorjamb. The VIN should match the one on the forward left corner of the dashboard. Missing or painted-over stickers may indicate prior accident repairs.

Front seating offers room for people more than 6 feet tall. This C320 Sport Coupe has the optional electrically adjustable leather seating, TouchShift transmission, TeleAid, and the Panorama sunroof.

Examine the attaching bolts for the radiator core support. There have been reports of the bolt heads breaking off.

The rear fold-down seats are split 60/40. The rear leg and head-room spaces are limited, but two average-size adults can ride comfortably. With 38.1 cubic feet of capacity when the seats are folded, there is a surprising amount of room available.

The V-6 is a tight fit; however, neat packaging means everything is easily accessible. Take a look at the bolt heads for the radiator core support. There have been some reports of bolt heads breaking off. Look for fluid leaks and check the radiators for any signs that the plastic end tanks or hose necks leak.

Common Parts List:
W203 C320 Sport Coupe, 2003–on

Engine:

Oil filter	$18.50
Fuel filter	$109.00
Starter	$253.75 (rebuilt)
Alternator (120 amp)	$575.30 (rebuilt)
Radiator	$332.00
Water pump	$206.00

Body:

Hood	$470.00
Left front fender	$230.00
Right rear quarter panel	$368.00
Rear bumper	$378.00
Windshield	$352.00
Headlight assembly:	
Standard	$350.00
Gas-discharge Xenon	$1,250.00
Taillight lens	$152.00

Exhaust:

Catalytic converter:	
Left (including front pipe)	$1,630.00
Right (including front pipe):	$1,630.00
Oxygen sensor:	
Front:	
Left	$165.00
Right	$159.00
Rear	$165.00

Chassis:

Vacuum brake booster:	$444.00
Brake fluid reservoir	$43.00
Front rotor	$52.00 each
Front pads (set)	$71.00
Front shocks:	
Standard	$152.00 each
Sport	$119.00 each
Rear shocks (sport)	$119.00 each

Manufacturers' stickers for SRS, vehicle data, and VIN are located in the driver's doorjamb. Confirm that the VIN matches with the VIN on the left front corner of the dashboard. Missing stickers may be a sign of prior accident repairs.

Common Parts List:
W203 C230 Kompressor, 2002–on

Engine:

Oil filter	$9.75
Fuel filter	$38.00
Fuel pump(s)	$197.00
Starter	$316.00 (rebuilt)
Alternator	$710.00
Radiator	$332.00
Fan clutch	$167.00
Water pump	$184.00

Body:

Front bumper:	
1999–2001 (w/o Parktronic)	$268.00
2002–on (not w/headlt washer)	$360.00
Hood	$470.00
Left front fender:	
1999–2001	$175.00
2002–on	$230.00
Right rear quarter panel	$368.00
Rear bumper:	
1999–2001:	
w/o impact strip	$428.00
only w/Parktronic	$306.00
w/o Parktronic	$290.00
2002–on:	$378.00
Headlight assembly:	
Standard	$350.00
Gas-discharge Xenon	$1,250.00
Taillight lens	$152.00

Exhaust:

Catalytic converter	$1,830.00
Muffler	$535.00
Oxygen sensor:	
after catalyst	$157.00
before catalyst	$157.00

Chassis:

Vacuum brake booster:	$444.00
Brake fluid reservoir	$43.00
Front rotor:	$47.50 each
1999–2000	$47.50 each
2002–on	$52.00 each
Front pads (set):	
1999–2001	$65.00
2002–on	$71.00
Front shocks:	
Standard	$152.00 each
Sport	$119.00 each
Rear shocks (sport)	$119.00 each

Technical Specifications:
W203 C320 Sport Coupe, 2003–on

Engine:

Type	SOHC, 90-degree V-6, three valves per cylinder
Displacement cc/ci	3199/195.2
Compression ratio	10.0:1
Bhp @ rpm	215 @ 5,700
Torque ft-lb @ rpm	221 @ 3,000–4,600
Injection	Sequential fuel injection, electronic throttle control, two-stage resonance intake manifold
Engine management	ME 2.8 w/phase-shifted twin spark plugs and twin coils per cylinder.
Fuel requirement	Premium unleaded

Chassis/drivetrain:

Transmission:	
Standard	Six-speed manual standard
Optional	Five-speed automatic w/driver-adaptive shift logic and Touch Shift
Steering	Rack-and-pinion, speed-sensitive hydraulic power-assist
Front suspension	Twin lower links, strut, coil springs, gas-charged twin-tube shocks, anti-roll bar
Rear suspension	Five-link, coil springs, gas-charged shocks, anti-roll bar
Differential:	
Automatic	3.27:1
Manual	3.46:1

General:

Wheelbase	106.9
Weight: (pounds)	
Automatic	3,415
Manual	3,385
Wheels	Alloy, 17x7.5
Tires	225/45ZR17
Brake system:	Hydraulic power-assisted, four-wheel discs w/four-channel ABS and Brake Assist and electronic brake proportioning.
Front	11.8-inch vented discs
Rear	11.4-inch vented discs
0–60 mph:	
Automatic	6.9 sec
Manual	6.8 sec
Maximum speed mph	130 (electronically limited)
Fuel economy:	
EPA estimated mpg	city/highway
Automatic	20/26
Manual	19/26

Rating Chart
W203 C230K/C320, 2002–on

Model	Comfort/Amenities	Reliability	Collectibility	Parts/Service Availability	Est. Annual Repair Costs
C230K	★★★⯪	★★★⯪	★★	★★★⯪	★★★
C320	★★★★	★★★⯪	★★	★★★⯪	★★★

Technical Specifications: W203 C230 Kompressor Sport Coupe, 2002–2004

Engine:

Type	Roots-type supercharger w/intercooler, inline four, DOHC, four valves/cylinder
Displacement cc/ci:	
2002	2,295/140
2003–2004	1,796/109.6
Compression ratio:	
2002	9.0:1
2003–2004	8.7:1
Bhp @ rpm:	
2002	192 @ 5,500
2003–2004	189 @ 5,800
Torque ft-lb @ rpm:	
2002	200 @ 2,500–4,800
2003–2004	192 @ 3,500–4,000
Engine management	SIM 4 sequential fuel injection
Fuel requirement	Premium unleaded

Chassis/drivetrain:

Transmission:	
Standard: 2002–2004	Six-speed manual standard
Optional: 2002–2004	Five-speed automatic w/driver-adaptive shift logic and Touch Shift
Steering	Rack-and-pinion, speed-sensitive hydraulic power assist
Front suspension	Twin lower links. Strut, coil springs, gas-charged twin-tube shocks, anti-roll bar
Rear suspension	Five-link, coil springs, gas-charged shocks, anti-roll bar
Differential:	
2002–2004:	
Automatic	3.27:1
Manual	3.46:1

General:

Wheelbase	106.9
Weight:	
Automatic:	
2002	3,360
2003–2004	3,280
Manual:	
2002	3,310 pounds
2003–2004	3,250
Wheels:	
2002:	
Standard	Alloy, 16x7.0, 10-spoke
Optional sport pkg.	Alloy, 17x7.5, 7-spoke
2003:	
Standard	Alloy, 16x7.0
Optional	Alloy, 17x7.5
2004:	Alloy, 17x7.5
Tires:	
2002–2003:	
Standard	205/55R16
Optional sport pkg.	225/45R17
2004:	225/45R17
Brake system:	Hydraulic power-assisted, four-wheel discs w/four-channel ABS and brake assist
2002:	
Front	11.8-inch vented discs
Rear	11.4-inch solid discs
Rear (2003-on)	11.4-inch vented discs
0–60 mph:	
2002–2004:	
Automatic	7.5 sec
Manual	7.2 sec
Maximum speed mph	130 electronically limited
Fuel economy:	
EPA estimated mpg:	city/highway
2002:	
Automatic	21/28
Manual	19/29
2003:	
Automatic	23/32
Manual	21/31
2004:	
Automatic	23/30
Manual	22/30

Electric and heated seats—If equipped, confirm that the seat heaters function and that the electrically operated seats work. Check the seat memory settings and confirm that the memory function works.

Radio—Check for poor radio reception. In some cars, the antenna amplifier is loose and degrades reception. If you hear popping or thumping in the speakers, there is an updated amplifier for the Bose systems that addresses the problem.

Panorama sunroof—Cycle through complete functions while idling and while on the test drive. Make sure the shades work and that the sunroof opens and closes.

Electronic key modules—Check all the function electronic key. There have been some reports responding to the lock/unlock and alarm func

Wind noise—Listen for wind noise from door s

Electric windows—Cycle windows multiple times to confirm they work correctly.

Rattles and squeaks—Listen for various rattles during the test drive. It could be as simple as screws/latches that have come loose or are improperly installed. It could also be a legacy of repairs from larger issues.

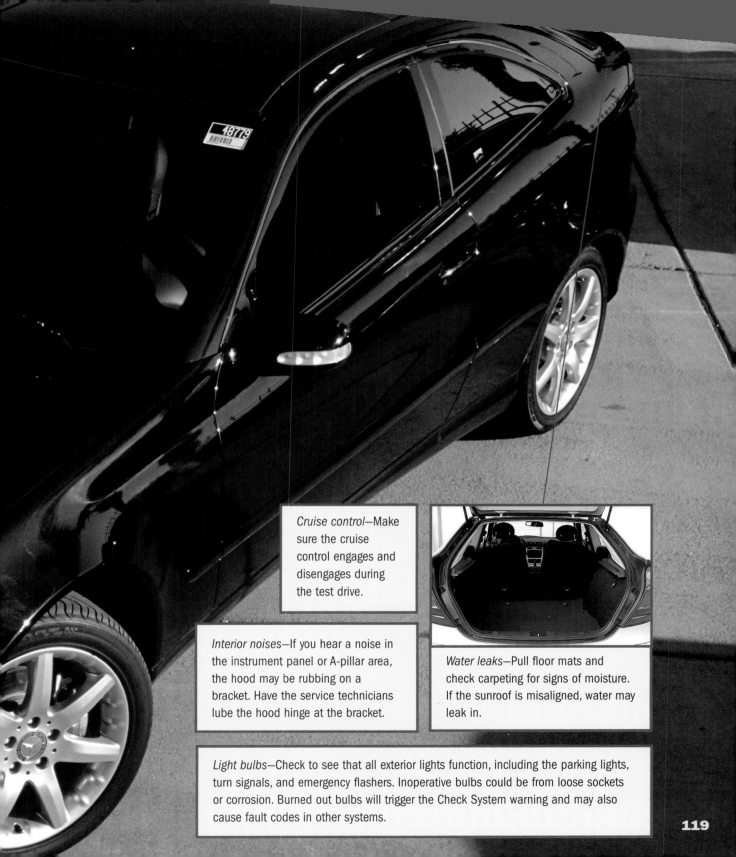

Cruise control—Make sure the cruise control engages and disengages during the test drive.

Interior noises—If you hear a noise in the instrument panel or A-pillar area, the hood may be rubbing on a bracket. Have the service technicians lube the hood hinge at the bracket.

Water leaks—Pull floor mats and check carpeting for signs of moisture. If the sunroof is misaligned, water may leak in.

Light bulbs—Check to see that all exterior lights function, including the parking lights, turn signals, and emergency flashers. Inoperative bulbs could be from loose sockets or corrosion. Burned out bulbs will trigger the Check System warning and may also cause fault codes in other systems.

Chapter 9

W124 300CE/ E320: 1988–1995

Basic History

The W124 became the benchmark for luxury cars from the Japanese manufacturers. Mercedes-Benz had to go head-to-head with these manufacturers if they had any hope of succeeding.

Shown to the public at the 1987 Geneva show, the W124 coupe went into production in 1988. The 300CE was powered by a 3.0-liter SOHC inline six and combined renowned Mercedes-Benz solid build quality in a more sporty looking coupe body. While the previous generation coupe had served well, the new coupe came to market with a more aerodynamic design, improved ergonomics for the occupants, and more up-to-date engines, suspensions, and brakes.

With the new chassis, Mercedes-Benz returned to its tradition of offering sedans, coupes, and convertibles based on the same platform. This was something they had not done since production of the W111 280SE coupes and convertibles that ended in 1971.

The convertibles became available in late 1992 as 1993 models, and owing to their limited production numbers, were declared collectible almost immediately. They were intended as a small production run, and the exclusivity of the convertible and the extra effort it took to engineer the car meant they were expensive and retailed for just under $80,000 in 1993.

The convertibles received reinforced A-pillars and windshield frames, as well as additional reinforcements to the side rails. The storage well for the soft top is a steel box, which also serves to reinforce the rear cowl area. The floorboards were doubled and a pressure-cast aluminum crossmember was placed inside the front cowl for more support.

To reduce cowl shake, a complex system of dampers was installed inside the windshield frame, behind each rear wheel, and on top of the left front shock. In addition, the engine mounts were specifically engineered to further reduce vibrations.

Ultimately, in order to remove the coupe's top sheet metal, which weighed about 65 pounds, an additional 285 pounds of reinforcements were installed. The results were worth the effort because the combination of strengthened windshield header and innovative rear pop-up headrests offered the same protective rollover strength as the coupe.

Sharing major mechanicals with the sedan, the coupes and convertibles ride on a wheelbase that is 3.3 inches shorter than the sedan. The doors are longer for easy rear seat entry and exit. Other than a rear anti-roll bar that is smaller than the sedans, the suspension and brakes are identical.

The front suspension was made up of modified MacPherson struts along with coil springs, gas-shocks, and an anti-roll bar. In the rear, Mercedes-Benz's patented multi-link design with coil springs and tube shocks were used. Brakes were power-assisted four-wheel discs with ABS.

During production, the W124 coupes and convertibles saw several running changes. Between introduction in 1987 through 1989, an SOHC 3.0-liter inline six engine powered the cars. In 1990, the engine was upgraded to a new design DOHC four-valve six. Featuring an aluminum crossflow head and variable valve timing, 217 brake horsepower was now available to drivers. As silky smooth and powerful as it was, more was to come when the engine was enlarged to 3.2 liters in 1993. Although brake horsepower remained the same, torque was raised from 195 to 229 foot-pounds.

With the changeover to the DOHC six in 1991, the transmissions were reprogrammed to start in low gear instead of second gear. The rear axle ratios were raised at the same time.

The transmission choices were limited to a four-speed automatic and an optional five-speed manual. Very few cars were ordered with the manual transmission, and finding a car with one would be surprising.

There were two changes, one cosmetic and one not, that happened in 1994. Across the board, Mercedes-Benz realigned the model designations of all their cars and switched from numeric-alphabetic designations to alphabetic-numeric (300CE to E320). In the case of the W124, this also meant changing the designation to reflect the enlarged 3.2-liter engine.

The E-Class models received a cosmetic facelift. The hood and grille contours were altered, headlights were updated to look more like their European counterparts, and the familiar star logo was changed from upright to flat against the hood.

The bumpers and body cladding were done in complementary colors. In 1995, the available color choices were reduced, and several had the cladding colored to match the rest of the car.

With no B pillar to anchor the front shoulder belts, Mercedes-Benz used motorized seatbelt extenders to propel the shoulder harness outward toward the driver and passenger, which presented the seatbelts in a convenient spot outboard of the front seat occupants' shoulders.

The interior design follows the Mercedes-Benz tradition of being logically laid out and well appointed. The instrument cluster is made up of three analog gauges with the speedometer in the center, a tachometer and analog clock to the right, and a combined water temperature, gas, and ammeter gauge to the left. The climate control system controls, located in the center console, are operated by a series of pushbuttons, rocker switches, and a rotating knob to set the temperature. Various system-warning lights are located in a row at the bottom of the cluster.

Check the climate control system closely as there have been many reported problems with air-flaps, compressors, and switch pad. Below the HVAC controls is the Becker GP radio, which is integrated with the vehicle alarm. If the radio is stolen, it renders itself useless without the correct code to re-enable it. Be sure to ask the seller for this code. Do not be surprised to see an aftermarket replacement radio because the original equipment radios were problematic and many have been replaced.

The shift lever is located in the center console with the control switches for the windows toward the rear of the console. Look for window control switches that have "sunk" into the center console, which indicates that the plastic underneath has broken. The switches should be above the burl wood. A replacement for the burl wood piece is in the range of $500 plus labor for installation. Also, because the wood patterns are unique, it will rarely match with the rest of the center console. To replace everything properly also means the ashtray piece should be replaced at the same time.

Electric control switches for the front seats are mounted on the doors. A programmable memory function allows multiple drivers to store their favorite seating and steering wheel position. Be certain to check the functions because these door-mounted switches are prone to breaking.

The front seat backs are scalloped to make additional room for the rear passengers' legs. A vacuum-operated system locks the seat backs in the upright position when the doors are closed and the engine is running. Seating options included heated front seats and orthopedic seats with inflatable and adjustable lumbar supports

M-B Tex upholstery was standard with leather and velour upholstery optional. The velour is rare because not many were ordered. The front armrest opens and offers storage for an optional cellular phone. Zebrano wood trim accents the dash and was extended to the doors for 1990.

The rear seating is cozy. There is a small stowage bin between the seats and a fold-down center armrest. Individual headrests and an electrically controlled roll-up sunscreen ensured passengers were comfortable and safe.

A driver side airbag was standard equipment, and starting in 1990, a passenger side airbag was optional. The passenger airbag later became standard equipment.

To protect convertible occupants, the rear seat headrests double as roll-over protection. Similar to the pop-up roll bar in the SLs, the rear headrests are hydraulically activated and, through a series of sensors, are deployed in 0.3 seconds. They can also be deployed manually through a console-mounted switch.

The complex convertible top uses an electrical pump, 10 switches, 7 solenoids, and 8 hydraulic cylinders. It can be raised or lowered in about 25 to 30 seconds, but only if the car is moving less than 6 miles per hour. The padded roof is an inch thick and has a glass rear window. When folded, the top takes up 3 cubic feet of trunk space.

Options included Acceleration Skid Control (ASR), which electronically reduces power or momentarily applies braking individually to the rear wheels to control wheel spin.

Overall, the W124 coupe and convertibles are possibly some of the best cars of their genre. Production ended in late 1995 as the next generation CLK was nearly ready for the marketplace. Convertibles will hold their value over the coupes. The DOHC cars offer more power. The optimum example is a 3.2-liter convertible.

Left: **The VIN stickers are attached in several places. This one is located underneath the right rear corner of the rear bumper surround in a recessed area. There should also be one under the front bumper in a similar recess. Missing stickers may mean a part was replaced or repaired.**

Middle, left: **The convertible top storage compartment intrudes into the trunk space and reduces it by 3 cubic feet. Nicely appointed, the spare tire is stored underneath the carpeted trunk floor.**

Bottom, left: **The convertible top is stowed beneath the nicely finished cover. The rear headrests are actually rollover bars that deploy automatically if sensors detect a collision or potential rollover. Note the right-side rearview mirror is larger than the left-side mirror.**

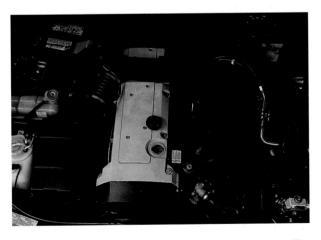

Above: **There are a couple of items to note in this photo. The rocker arm is visible through the oil filler hole in the valve cover, which is aluminum-colored. This tells the buyer that the previous owners changed the oil regularly. The insulation for the airflow meter wiring harness has deteriorated from the underhood heat. Check this carefully, because a replacement will cost between $300 and $800, depending on the car.**

The flush-mounted headlights are kept clean by wipers. An A-pillar design channels rainwater up and away from the side glass. Look underneath the front bumper for the VIN sticker. If it is not there, it may mean the bumper has been repainted or replaced.

The headroom and legroom for the rear-seat occupants are at a premium. Otherwise, the accommodations are luxurious.

Technical Specifications: W124 E320 Coupes & Convertibles, 1994–1995

Engine:

Type	DOHC, inline six, four valves per cylinder
Displacement cc/ci	3,199/195.1
Compression ratio	10.0:1
Bhp @ rpm	217 @ 5,500
Torque ft-lb @ rpm	229 @ 3,750
Injection type	Bosch, HFM w/port fuel injection
Fuel requirement	Premium unleaded, 91 octane

Chassis/drivetrain:

Transmission	Four-speed automatic
Steering	Recirculating ball, power-assisted
Front suspension	Modified MacPherson struts, lower A-arms, coil springs, tube shocks, anti-roll bar
Rear suspension	Five-link, coil springs, tube shocks, anti-roll bar
Differential	2.65:1

General:

Wheelbase	106.9
Weight	4,055
Wheels	15x6.5J, alloy
Tires	195/65R-15
Brake system:	Four-wheel disc, vacuum-assisted, ABS
Front	11.2-inch vented discs
Rear	10.2-inch solid discs
0–60 mph	8.7 sec
Maximum speed mph	130 (est.)
Fuel economy:	city/hwy
EPA estimated mpg	18/23

This space-saver spare is stored below the carpeted floor mat. Confirm that the jack and tool roll are present and accounted for, because replacing them is not cheap.

Common Parts List: W124 300CE Coupes & Cabriolets, 1988–1993

Engine:

Oil filter	$9.75
Fuel filter	$42.50
Fuel pump(s) (two per car)	$252.00 each
Starter:	$229.00 (rebuilt)
Chassis type 124.050/052	$229.00 (rebuilt)
Chassis type 124.066 (conv)	$222.00 (rebuilt)
Alternator:	$319.00 (rebuilt)
90 amp	$354.00 (rebuilt)
Radiator	$184.00
Fan clutch	$177.00
Water pump	$360.00 (w/seals)

Body:

Front bumper:	
Coupe (124.050)	$690.00
Coupe (124.052)	$498.00
Convertible (124.066)	$498.00
Hood:	$448.00
Coupe	$448.00
Convertible (124.066)	$525.00
Left front fender (Coupe/Conv)	$266.00
Rear bumper:	
Coupe (124.050)	$675.00
Coupe (124.052)	$630.00
Convertible (124.066)	$630.00
Windshield	$362.00
Headlight assembly	$358.00
Taillight lens	$110.00

Exhaust:

Catalytic converter (including front pipe)	$2,710.00
Center muffler	$322.00
Rear muffler	$192.00
Oxygen sensor	$178.00

Chassis:

Brake master:	
to 6/94	$270.00
from 6/94	S204.00
Front rotor:	
Chassis type 124.050	$52.00 each
Chassis type 124.052/066	$61.00 each
Front pads (set):	
Chassis type 124.050	$53.00
Chassis type 124.052/066	$77.00
Front shocks:	$230.00 each
Coupe (124.050/052)	$230.00 each
Convertible (124.066)	$218.00 each
Rear shocks:	
Coupe (124.050/052)	$114.00 each
Convertible (124.066)	$97.00 each

Common Parts List: W124 E320 Coupe & Cabriolets, 1994–1995

Engine:

Oil filter	$9.75
Fuel filter	$42.50
Fuel pump(s) (two per car)	$252.00 each
Starter	$222.00 (rebuilt)
Alternator:	$262.00 (rebuilt)
90 amp	$354.00 (rebuilt)
Radiator	$184.00
Fan clutch	$177.00
Water pump	$360.00 w/seals

Body:

Front bumper	$498.00
Hood:	
Coupe through 1993 (124.052)	$448.00
Coupe from 1993 (124.052)	$525.00
Convertible	$525.00
Left front fender	$266.00
Right rear quarter panel:	
Coupe	$655.00
Cabriolet	$2,020.00
Rear bumper	$630.00
Windshield	$362.00
Headlight assembly	$358.00
Taillight lens	$110.00

Exhaust:

Catalytic converter (including front pipe)	$1,760.00
Center muffler	$282.00
Rear muffler	$320.00
Oxygen sensor	$129.00

Chassis:

Brake master:	
to 6/94	$270.00
from 6/94	$204.00
Front rotor	$61.00 each
Front pads (set)	$77.00
Front shocks:	
Coupe (124.052)	$230.00 each
Standard	$230.00 each
Heavy duty	$212.00 each
Sport	$218.00 each
Convertible: (124.066)	
Heavy duty	$212.00 each
Sport	$218.00 each
Rear shocks:	$114.00 each
Coupe	$114.00 each
Convertible	$97.00 each

Rating Chart: W124 300E/E320 Coupes & Convertibles, 1988–1995

Model	Comfort/Amenities	Reliability	Collectibility	Parts/Service Availability	Est. Annual Repair Costs
300E Coupe	★★★★	★★★★	★★★	★★★★	★★★
300E Conv.	★★★★	★★★★	★★★	★★★★	★★★
E32 Coupe	★★★★	★★★★	★★★	★★★★	★★★
E320 Conv.	★★★★	★★★★	★★★	★★★★	★★★

Technical Specifications: W124 300CE Coupes & Convertibles, 1988–1992

Engine:

Type:

1988–1989	SOHC, inline six, two valves per cylinder
1990–1992	DOHC, inline six, four valves per cylinder

Displacement cc/ci:

1988–1989	2,962/181
1990–1992	2,962/181

Compression ratio:

1988–1989	9.2:1
1990–1992	10.0:1

Bhp @ rpm:

1988–1989	177 @ 5,700
1990–1992	217 @ 6,400

Torque ft-lb @ rpm:

1988–1989	188 @ 4,400
1990–1992	195 @ 4,600

Injection type:

1988–1989	Bosch KE Jetronic
1990–1992	Bosch KE-5 electrical, port injection

Fuel requirement — Premium unleaded, 91 octane

Chassis/drivetrain:

Transmission	Four-speed automatic
Steering	Recirculating ball, power-assisted
Front suspension	Modified MacPherson struts, lower A-arms, coil springs, tube shocks, anti-roll bar.
Rear suspension	Multilink, coil springs, tube shocks, anti-roll bar
Differential	3.27:1

General:

Wheelbase	106.9 in

Weight:

Cabrio	4,018 (est.)
Coupe	3,645
Wheels	15x6.5J
Tires	195/65ZR-15
Brake system:	Four-wheel disc, vacuum-assisted, ABS
Front	11.2-inch vented discs
Rear	10.2-inch solid discs

0–60 mph:

1988–1989	8.3 sec
1990–1993	8.5 sec

Maximum speed mph:

1988–1989	140 (est.)
1990–1993	140 (est.)

Fuel economy: city/hwy

EPA estimated mpg:

1988–1989	17/23
1990–1993	17/21

Rubber differential mounts—Inspect the mounts for cracks and breaks. Listen for a "thump" when engaging the drive or a thump on deceleration. This is the usual indication of deteriorated mounts.

VIN tags—Check for the barcode tag behind the license plate (trunk). Also check both bumpers for the presence or absence of VIN tags. This indicates refinishing or replacement and may indicate crash damage, so check other panels. On 1993 and earlier cars, the VIN tags were on panels. The 1994 and later models don't have them.

Airflow sensor wiring harness—Look at the wiring harness that goes to the airflow sensor. Check for deteriorated insulation, which is common because it is in an area where heat from the engine dries the insulation. The harness is about $500 and two hours of labor.

Fuel pumps—Listen for noisy pumps. If you can hear them inside the car with the engine running, a replacement is needed. Two of them cost around $200 each plus labor.

Head gasket—Look for oil leaking on the right side of the engine. This is usually a sign of a head gasket leak. The replacement part isn't all that expensive, but figure at least eight hours of labor.

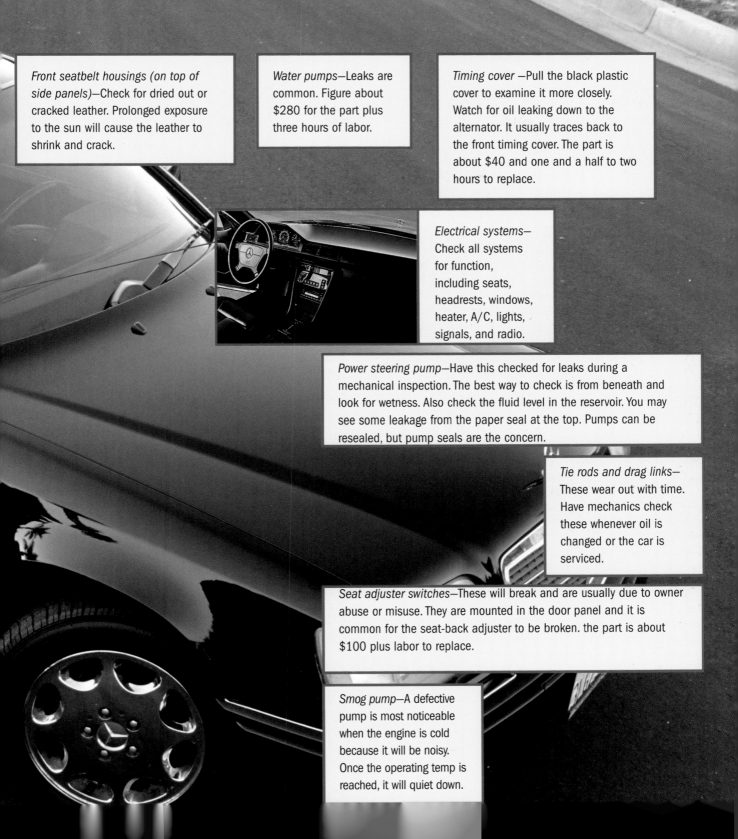

Front seatbelt housings (on top of side panels)—Check for dried out or cracked leather. Prolonged exposure to the sun will cause the leather to shrink and crack.

Water pumps—Leaks are common. Figure about $280 for the part plus three hours of labor.

Timing cover—Pull the black plastic cover to examine it more closely. Watch for oil leaking down to the alternator. It usually traces back to the front timing cover. The part is about $40 and one and a half to two hours to replace.

Electrical systems—Check all systems for function, including seats, headrests, windows, heater, A/C, lights, signals, and radio.

Power steering pump—Have this checked for leaks during a mechanical inspection. The best way to check is from beneath and look for wetness. Also check the fluid level in the reservoir. You may see some leakage from the paper seal at the top. Pumps can be resealed, but pump seals are the concern.

Tie rods and drag links—These wear out with time. Have mechanics check these whenever oil is changed or the car is serviced.

Seat adjuster switches—These will break and are usually due to owner abuse or misuse. They are mounted in the door panel and it is common for the seat-back adjuster to be broken. the part is about $100 plus labor to replace.

Smog pump—A defective pump is most noticeable when the engine is cold because it will be noisy. Once the operating temp is reached, it will quiet down.

Chapter 10

W208 CLK320/ CLK430/CLK55 AMG: 1998–2003*

Basic History

Note: The W208 convertibles continued to 2003 while waiting for the W209 chassis convertibles to be released.

In 1997, Mercedes-Benz introduced the CLK series of coupes. In departing from its tradition of sedan-derived coupes, the CLK coupes and convertibles were not directly derived from the C-class sedans. The new CLKs did use suspension components from the C-class and brakes from the E-class platforms. Although they shared the same 105.9-inch wheelbase of the C-class, all similarity stops there as the exterior and interiors are distinct and share no body panels with other cars.

Designed from the onset as a coupe, the wedge-shaped body features short front and rear overhangs and a gracefully sloping roofline. While the larger CL500 and CL600 coupes don't have a B-pillar, the CLK coupes have a fixed B-pillar and quarter windows. The high rear deck provides space for an 11-cubic foot trunk, and the rear seats are situated slightly higher than the front seats. Rear seat occupants will find decent leg and headroom, and those over 6 feet tall will find space at a premium.

When it was introduced, the CLK320 coupe came equipped with Electronic Stability Program (ESP) and Automatic Slip Control (ASR). Working in concert, ESP monitors vehicle responses to driver inputs and can reduce engine power or apply braking action at individual wheels to help correct understeer or oversteer. The ASR actively monitors for rear wheel spin and using the ESP system, it will reduce power or apply rear brakes to minimize slipping.

The coupe was joined in 1999 by a convertible that used the same 3.2-liter V-6- and a V-8-powered CLK430 coupe. The 4.3-liter convertible became available in 2000. The CLK55 AMG coupe was added in 2001 and was followed by a convertible version in 2002.

In developing the convertible version, reinforcements were incorporated into the body side members and drive-shaft tunnel. A crossmember was added under the front seats and the A-pillar. The truncated B-pillar was strengthened. The rear bulkhead is also reinforced and contains two pop-up head restraints that double as roll-over protection. Diagonal struts at the front and rear of the chassis tie together components such as the front suspension crossmember and the doorsill. A vibration damper is used up front to isolate and reduce cowl shake. Together, these reinforcements add up to an additional 500 pounds of weight. The extra engineering and effort also added between $6,000 and $8,000 to the price tag.

The W208 platform continued to introduce enhancements during its four-year production run. Brake Assist, a system that senses emergency braking and applies maximum brake boost to help reduce stopping distances, was added in 1999.

The Cockpit Management and Data System (COMAND), an integrated in-dash navigation system with a CD player and CD-ROM drive, added to the list of available options in 2000. The TeleAid GPS notification system was also added that year. TeleAid uses GPS satellites to pinpoint the location of the car and has a cellular phone link for 24/7 contact with a central support desk for information and to provide roadside and emergency support services. Designo edition interior packages were also added as options for the 2000 models.

Perhaps the most unique feature of the W208 is the SmartKey. It is an electronic key fob that uses infrared signals to remotely lock and unlock the car and open or close the windows and the optional sunroof. Unlike a normal key of the past, SmartKey, when inserted into the ignition switch, electronically unlocks the ignition and starts the car. Removing the SmartKey from the ignition electronically disables the engine computer. It is a fairly effective antitheft device. SmartKey enhancements in 2001 allowed up to three different SmartKey transmitters to be assigned to a car with each one linked to memory features for driver's seat, mirrors, and climate control preferences.

The CLK's engines were common to several other platforms. All are V configurations with alloy blocks and heads, electronic fuel injection with twin spark plugs, two intake and one exhaust valve per cylinder. The magnesium intake manifold incorporates two stages with variable length intake runners for improved throttle response.

The 5.5-liter V-8s in the CLK55 AMG coupe and convertibles are hand assembled and use traditional hot-rod techniques such as increased displacement, forged crankshaft, and an 8-millimeter longer stroke. Forged connecting rods and pistons, reworked cylinder heads with AMG specific camshafts and a reworked intake manifold are combined to produce 342 brake horsepower and 376 foot-pounds of torque. The result is 0-to-60 times in the 5.3-second range.

The transmissions for the CLK320 and CLK430 are the much-improved five-speed electronically controlled automatic. The CLK55 AMG transmission is borrowed from the V-12-powered cars. In addition, the AMG versions received TouchShift for improved shifts and allows gear changes to be made by a left-flick for upshifts and a right-flick for downshifts. The instrument cluster display shows which gear is selected. In all of the W208 CLK models, there is a driver-selectable winter mode that starts in second gear and a special second reverse gear to help on slippery surfaces.

The C-class suspension components are the starting point. Stiffer springs and gas-pressurized shocks complement the independent upper and lower A-arms in front and five-arm multilink rear suspension. The ride is firm but not out of character for a two-door sports coupe.

The brakes are four-wheel discs with ABS and Electronic Brake Force Distribution, which helps distribute the braking forces more evenly among the four wheels, and it works with ABS for quicker stopping.

Instrumentation includes an electronic analog speedometer, tachometer, fuel, coolant, oil pressure, and fuel economy readouts. The odometer, trip odometer, clock, and outside temperature are displayed in the center of the speedometer. Other displays include seatbelt warnings, exterior light bulb failures, brake system, front pad wear, SRS, ABS ASR/ESP, Brake Assist, engine electronics, and low fuel, oil, coolant, and washer indicators.

The Mercedes Flexible Service System (FSS) monitors driving conditions and displays distance remaining to the next routine maintenance services, such as oil changes.

The dual climate control system is CFC-free, and the controls are located in the center console. The system does have some limitations. The controls are not intuitive and some airflow combinations are impossible to achieve.

The multifunction steering wheel controls the radio, optional navigation system, onboard telephone, and dash displays. Power window controls are clustered on the driver-side door and have the popular one-touch control for raising and lowering.

The front seats are individual buckets with 10-way power controls and three memory positions. When the front seatbacks are released for rear-seat access, the seats slide forward. When the seatback is returned to the upright position, the seats automatically return to their original position.

Standard equipment included driver and front passenger airbags, side-impact airbags, leather upholstery, Electronic Stability Program (on the CLK430 and CLK55 AMG), walnut trim, and the SmartKey infrared key and security system. Airbags are provided for the driver and front seat passenger, and door-mounted side impact airbags, knee bolsters, and Emergency Tensioning Retractors (ETR) are also used to protect front seat occupants. Sensors are used to deactivate restraint systems for the seats not occupied. Mercedes-Benz's BabySmart system deactivates the front passenger airbag when a BabySmart compatible seat is used.

Options included a power sunroof, heated headlamp washers, heated front seats, multicontour front seats that could be individually optioned, integrated cell phone, a trunk mounted six-disc CD changer, metallic paint, Xenon gas-discharge headlights, rain sensing windshield wipers, and ESP for the CLK320.

The convertible top is made up of three layers; the inner liner, a 0.8-inch-thick layer of padding, and an outer layer. The top is not fully automatic. It has a manual release handle, but the rest of the raising or lowering is done automatically and takes about 30 seconds to complete. The rear glass is electrically heated. The convertible CLK trunk, at 9.4

cubic feet, loses about 1.5 cubic feet of trunk space to the coupe's 11.0 cubic feet of space. With the top down, trunk space is reduced to 5.7 cubic feet.

These cars are still fairly new and long-term maintenance trends have not shown up. The sophisticated electronics in these cars has led to a series of electrical problems with items such as malfunctioning electric window controls and brake light switches that fail and set off warning signals. Various exterior lights burn out sooner than expected, and the light-out warning messages can also cause other, interrelated systems to generate warning displays.

Be sure you review past maintenance records for patterns of failures and exercise all the car's electrical and mechanical systems to confirm they function correctly.

Long term, the convertible versions will continue their popularity over the coupes. The AMG versions will likely maintain a higher resale value, and the AMG convertibles will likely be the best value.

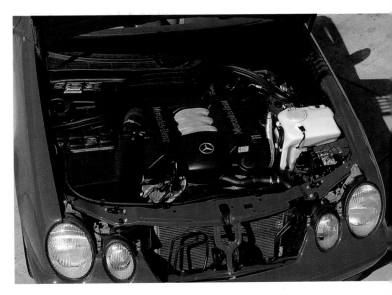

Check in and around the engine compartment for fluid leaks. Look for any overspray to indicate prior damage repairs.

The famous Mercedes-Benz star casts a shadow on the hood. Check the gaps between various panels for consistency and evenness. Also check for overspray, which may be an indication of prior repairs.

This is a closer look at the center console. The cupholder is located just in front of console storage bin. Spilled liquid can get into the shifter area and wreak havoc with the electrical switches.

The rear seating area is cozy and luxurious. The center armrest pivots down, and one of the sound system speakers is nestled below the armrest. Rear windscreen attaching points are on top of the side panels, just behind the shoulder harnesses.

At 9.4 cubic feet of storage space, the convertible's trunk is about 1.5 cubic feet less than the coupe's trunk. When the top is down, an additional 3.7 cubic feet is lost. Space-saver spare and battery are stored beneath the floor.

The Bordeaux Red color really accents the graceful lines of this 1998 CLK430 Coupe. Note the rearview mirrors on this car don't have the turn-signal repeaters. They came onboard later. Side skirts and bumper surrounds on the V-8-powered cars differ from the six-cylinder models.

The 4.3-liter V-8 is shrouded neatly. There are occasional reports of rodents getting underneath and damaging the electrical wiring. Be sure to have this checked during the prepurchase inspection. Look for signs of engine fluid or radiator leaks.

Release handles for the folding rear seats are the two red-labeled items at the top left and right of the trunk opening. The space-saver tire, jack, and battery are stored beneath the carpeted trunk mat. The CD changer is tucked into the right corner of the trunk.

The U.S. regulations require that the VIN be displayed on the dash of all vehicles. Most modern Mercedes have a similar sticker located in a similar area of the windshield. It should match the VIN sticker in the driver's doorjamb.

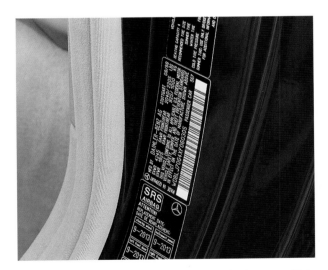

The driver-side doorjamb contains, top to bottom, a vehicle capacity sticker, manufacturers' VIN sticker, and SRS sticker. The sequence may vary from year to year and model to model, but one thing holds true—if these stickers are missing or are painted over, look closely for indications of damage repairs.

In true hot rod fashion, the technicians at AMG enlarged the V-8 to 5.5 liters. Hand assembled by the staff at AMG, 342 horsepower and 376 foot-pounds of torque are on tap for spirited drives.

Common Parts List: W208 CLK320 Cpe & Cab, 1998–2003*

NOTE: The W208 convertibles continued to M.Y. 2003 while waiting for the W209 chassis convertibles to be released.

Engine:

Oil filter	$18.50
Fuel filter	$109.00
Fuel pump(s)	$308.00
Starter	$253.75 (rebuilt)
Alternator	$272.00 (new)
Radiator	$288.00
Water pump	$360.00

Body:

Front bumper:	
Standard	$380.00
AMG style	
w/o headlight washers	$685.00
w/headlight washers	$720.00
Hood	$560.00
Left front fender	$234.00
Right rear quarter panel	$670.00
Rear bumper:	
Standard	$408.00
AMG styling pkg.	$1,220.00
Windshield:	
w/rain sensing	$418.00
w/o rain sensing	$330.00
Headlight assembly:	
Standard	$350.00
Gas-discharge Xenon	$885.00
Taillight assembly	$107.00

Exhaust:

Catalytic converter:	
Front pipe (including convertor):	
Left	$900.00
Right	$1,530.00
Intermediate pipe:	$750.00
Tailpipe extension	$65.00
Oxygen sensor:	
Front:	
Left	$158.35
Right	$158.35
Rear:	
Left	$210.00
Right	$200.00

Chassis:

Brake master	$224.00
Front rotor $75.00 each	
Front pads (set)	$72.00
Front shocks	$136.00 each
Rear shocks $119.00 each	

Common Parts List: W208 CLK430 Cpe & Cab, 1999–2003*

NOTE: The W208 convertibles continued to M.Y. 2003 while waiting for the W209 chassis convertibles to be released.

Engine:

Oil filter	$18.50
Fuel filter	$109.00
Fuel pump(s)	$197.00
Starter	$253.75 (rebuilt)
Alternator	$627.00 (rebuilt)
Radiator	$240.00
Fan clutch	$169.00
Water pump	$360.00

Body:

Front bumper:	
Standard	$380.00
AMG style:	
w/o headlight washers	$685.00
w/headlight washers	$720.00
Hood	$560.00
Left front fender	$234.00
Right rear quarter panel	$670.00
Rear bumper:	
Standard	$408.00
AMG styling pkg.	$1,220.00
Windshield:	
w/rain sensing	$418.00
w/o rain sensing	$330.00
Headlight assembly:	
Standard	$350.00
Gas-discharge Xenon	$885.00
Taillight assembly	$107.00

Exhaust:

Catalytic converter:	
Front pipe (including converter):	
Left	$2,110.00
Right	$2,110.00
Intermediate pipe:	
Coupe	$525.00
Convertible	$615.00
Rear muffler	$532.28
Oxygen sensor:	
Front:	
Left	$158.35
Right	$158.35
Rear:	
Left	$210.00
Right	$200.00

Chassis:

Brake master	$224.40
Front rotor	$75.00 each
Front pads (set)	$72.00
Front shocks	$136.00 each
Rear shocks	$119.00 each

Common Parts List: W208 CLK55 AMG Cpe & Cab, 2001–2003*

*NOTE: The W208 convertibles continued to M.Y. 2003 while waiting for the W209 chassis convertibles to be released.

Engine:

Oil filter	$18.50
Fuel filter	$109.00
Fuel pump(s)	$197.00
Starter	$253.75 (rebuilt)
Alternator	$627.00 (rebuilt)
Radiator	$240.00
Fan clutch	$169.00
Water pump	$360.00

Body:

Front bumper:	
w/o headlight washers	$685.00
w/headlight washers	$720.00
Hood	$560.00
Left front fender	$234.00
Right rear quarter panel	$670.00
Rear bumper	$1,220.00
Windshield:	
w/rain sensing	$418.00
w/o rain sensing	$330.00
Headlight assembly:	
Standard	$350.00
Gas-discharge Xenon	$885.00
Taillight assembly	$107.00

Exhaust:

Catalytic converter	
Front pipe (including converter):	
Left	$2,110.00
Right	$2,110.00
Intermediate pipe:	
Coupe	$525.00
Convertible	$615.00
Rear muffler	$532.28
Oxygen sensor:	
Front:	
Left	$158.35
Right	$158.35
Rear:	
Left	$210.00
Right	$200.00

Chassis:

Brake master	$245.00
Front rotor	$254.00 each
Front pads (set)	$216.00
Front shocks	$136.00 each
Rear shocks	$119.00 each

Rating Chart: W208 CLK's, 1998–2003*

*NOTE: The W208 convertibles continued to M.Y. 2003 while waiting for the W209 chassis convertibles to be released.

Model	Comfort/Amenities	Reliability	Collectibility	Parts/Service Availability	Est. Annual Repair Costs
CLK320 Coupe	★★★½	★★★½	★★★	★★★½	★★★
CLK320 Cab	★★★½	★★★½	★★★½	★★★½	★★★
CLK430 Coupe	★★★★	★★★½	★★★	★★★½	★★★
CLK430 Cab	★★★★	★★★½	★★★½	★★★½	★★★
CLK55AMG Coupe	★★★★	★★★½	★★★½	★★★½	★★★
CLK55AMG Cab	★★★★	★★★½	★★★½	★★★½	★★★

Technical Specifications: W208 CLK320, 1998–2003*

NOTE: The W208 convertibles continued to M.Y. 2003 while waiting for the W209 chassis convertibles to be released.

Engine:

Type	90-degree V-6, chain-driven SOHC per bank, two intake valves/one exhaust valve per cylinder
Displacement cc/ci	3,199/195
Compression ratio	10.0:1
Bhp @ rpm	215 @ 5,700
Torque ft-lb @ rpm	229 @ 3,000–4,600
Injection type	Sequential fuel injection, electronic throttle control, two-stage resonance intake manifold
Engine management	ME 2.8 engine control w/phase-shifted twin sparkplugs per cylinder, two coils per cylinder
Fuel requirement	Premium unleaded, 91 pump octane

Chassis/drivetrain:

Transmission	Five-speed electronically controlled automatic w/driver-adaptive shift logic
Steering	Recirculating ball, hydraulic power-assisted
Front suspension	Double wishbone, coil springs, gas-charged shocks, anti-roll bar, anti-lift and anti-dive geometry
Rear suspension	Five-link, coil springs, gas-charged shocks, anti-roll bar, anti-lift and anti-squat geometry
Differential	3.07:1

General:

Wheelbase	105.9
Weight:	
Coupe	3,265
Cabrio	3,650
Wheels:	
Front	16x7.0 alloy
Optional	17x7.5 alloy
Rear	16x7.0 alloy
Optional	17x8.5 alloy
Tires:	
Front	205/55R16 all-season
Optional	225/45ZR17
Rear	205/55R16 all-season
Optional	245/40ZR17
Brake system:	Hydraulic power-assisted four-wheel discs w/four-channel ABS
Front	11.8-inch vented discs
Rear	11.4-inch solid discs
0–60 mph:	
Coupe	6.9 sec
Cabrio	7.7 sec
Maximum speed mph	130 mph (electronically limited)
Fuel economy:	city/hwy
EPA estimated mpg:	
Coupe	20/27
Cabrio	19/26

Technical Specifications:
W208 CLK430, 1999–2003*

NOTE: The W208 convertibles continued to M.Y. 2003 while waiting for the W209 chassis convertibles to be released.

Engine:

Type	90-degree V-8, chain-driven SOHC per bank, two intake valves/one exhaust valve per cylinder
Displacement cc/ci	4,266/260.3
Compression ratio	10.0:1
Bhp @ rpm	275 @ 5,750
Torque ft-lb @ rpm	295 @ 3,000–4,600
Injection type	Sequential fuel injection, electronic throttle control, two-stage resonance intake manifold
Engine management	ME 2.8 engine control w/phase-shifted twin sparkplugs per cylinder, two coils per cylinder
Fuel requirement	Premium unleaded, 91 pump octane

Chassis/drivetrain:

Transmission	Five-speed electronically controlled automatic w/driver-adaptive shift logic
Steering	Recirculating ball, hydraulic power-assist
Front suspension	Double wishbone, coil springs, gas-charged shocks, anti-roll bar, anti-lift and anti-dive geometry
Rear suspension	Five-link, coil springs, gas-charged shocks, anti-roll bar, anti-lift and anti-squat geometry
Differential	2.87:1

General:

Wheelbase	105.9
Weight:	
Coupe	3,365
Cabrio:	3,745
Wheels:	
Front	17x7.5 alloy
Rear	17x8.5 alloy
Tires:	
Front	225/45ZR17
Rear	245/40ZR17
Brake system:	Hydraulic power-assisted four-wheel discs w/four-channel ABS
Front	11.8-inch vented discs
Rear	11.4-inch solid discs
0–60 mph:	
Coupe	6.1 sec
Cabrio	6.9 sec
Maximum speed mph	130 mph (electronically limited)
Fuel economy:	city/hwy
EPA estimated mpg:	
Coupe	18/24
Cabrio	17/24

Technical Specifications:
W208 CLK55 AMG, 2001–2003

NOTE: The W208 convertibles continued to M.Y. 2003 while waiting for the W209 chassis convertibles to be released.

Engine:

Type	90-degree V-8, chain-driven SOHC per bank, two intake valves/one exhaust valve per cylinder
Displacement cc/ci	5,439/331.9
Compression ratio	10.5:1
Bhp @ rpm	342 @ 5,500
Torque ft-lb @ rpm	376 @ 3,000
Injection type	Sequential fuel injection, electronic throttle control, two-stage resonance intake manifold
Engine management	ME 2.8 engine control w/phase-shifted twin sparkplugs per cylinder, two coils per cylinder
Fuel requirement	Premium unleaded, 91 pump octane

Chassis/drivetrain:

Transmission	Five-speed electronically controlled automatic w/driver-adaptive shift logic
Steering	Recirculating ball, hydraulic power-assist
Front suspension	Double wishbone, coil springs, gas-charged shocks, anti-roll bar, anti-lift and anti-dive geometry
Rear suspension	Five-link, coil springs, gas-charged shocks, anti-roll bar, anti-lift and anti-squat geometry
Differential	2.82:1

General:

Wheelbase	105.9
Weight:	
Coupe	3,485
Cabrio	3,845
Wheels:	
Front	17x7.5 multipiece alloy
Rear	17x8.5 multipiece alloy
Tires:	
Front	225/45ZR17
Rear	245/40ZR17
Brake system:	Hydraulic power-assisted four-wheel discs w/four-channel ABS
Front	13.2-inch vented discs
Rear	11.8-inch vented discs
0–60 mph	4.9 sec
Maximum speed mph	155 (electronically limited)
Fuel economy:	city/hwy
EPA estimated mpg:	
Coupe	17/24
Cabrio	16/22

Dashboard—Look closely around the dash air vents and the passenger airbag cover for any signs of cracking.

Windows—Pull mats and check carpet for dampness due to leaky windows. Frameless windows are notorious for not sealing properly. If there are any problems with the window not sealing tightly, water could leak in.

Transmission—Spilled drinks in the center console can allow fluids to seep down into the shift quadrant area. Moisture getting into the electronic switch for the transmission can cause all sorts of problems up to and including complete shutdown.

Steering wheel buttons—Check to make sure the steering wheel buttons function properly and control the radio and message displays.

Power windows—There have been a lot of problems reported with malfunctioning power windows that don't respond to express up/down. Be sure to cycle windows multiple times during the test drive and review maintenance records for repairs.

Crank pulley—Check for cracks.

Rear differential—Check for oil leaks.

Motor mounts—Check to make sure they have not broken or failed.

Fuel tank sending units—There have been multiple reports of gas gauges not registering correctly. It could be a bad sending unit or a bad gauge. Check each time the car is filled up to confirm the reading is correct.

Catalytic converters—Some instances of the catalytic converters failing prematurely were reported. This makes a rattling noise. The problem seems to affect cars built prior to 2003. MB has since switched suppliers. No known TSB. If you hear a rattle in the exhaust, it might be worth having the MB service folks check into it. Converters are warranty items and if failure occurs within the first 50,000 miles, a replacement may be covered under warranty.

Creaks when traversing driveways—Some CLK430s exhibit creaking when going in/out of driveways. Check the aerodynamic side-skirts on the doors, fenders, and sills—they may be touching slightly.

Dash display—There have been reports of the LCD displays, such as the mileage or clock, dropping pixels. The only way to repair this is to remove and replace the instrument cluster. The LCDs are not serviceable. If the car is out of warranty, it's on your pocketbook.

Chapter 11

W126 380SEC/ 500SEC/560SEC: 1982–1991
Basic History

With its flowing and functional design, the W126 S-class is the first Mercedes-Benz to be designed under the guidance of chief stylist Bruno Sacco. The 380SEC signaled a return to the Mercedes-Benz tradition of basing its top-of-the-line coupe on the luxury sedans. The coupe was released in 1982, two years after the introduction of the S-class sedans, and took the place of the 450SLC derivative of the W107 SL roadster. While based on the W126 S-class chassis and running gear, the coupes are 3.3 inches shorter than the short-wheelbase sedan.

Although these cars don't share any panels with the W126 S-class sedans, the family resemblance is obvious. The front of the car uses the flatter, SL-type grille treatment with the Mercedes-Benz star prominently displayed in the center. The headlights are nestled in alongside the grille, and are perhaps not quite as smooth as the more integrated European lighting. The windshield, that is the same as the sedans, is more steeply raked and flows gracefully into the roofline.

The bumpers were far better integrated into the overall design and are visually more appealing. Following the line of the bumpers from front to rear, the side body cladding is color-matched to the bumpers and accentuates the front-to-rear look and protects the lower body from rock chips and parking lot dings. The door handles are nicely streamlined, and the fairing that leads to them also keeps the handles clean during inclement weather.

The rain gutters channel water up over the roof and help keep the side windows clear during wet weather. The roof panel is styled to direct water to the rear window surround, which is designed to catch water and guide it around the trunk opening and empty at the center above the license plate. All this helps keep the taillight lenses clear of dirt and debris.

The all-aluminum 3.8-liter V-8 produced 155 brake horsepower at 4,750 rpm. The SOHC design used single-row chain drives for the overhead camshafts. Unfortunately, these single-row chains are prone to stretch, particularly if the engine oil is not changed regularly, which can lead to the chain jumping a tooth. When this occurs, the usual result is valve-to-piston contact and substantial and serious engine damage. The single-row timing chains were discontinued in 1983, and double-row chains were used from 1984 on. Many of the 3.8-liter engines have been retrofitted with an updated design during normal rebuilds. Review the maintenance records to see if this fix has been performed. It is expensive, but once it is done, the problem can no longer happen.

In 1984, the 3.8-liter engine was replaced by a 4,973-cc, 303.5-ci V-8 that produced 184 brake horsepower at 4,500 rpm. In some respects, Mercedes responded to the gray-market demand for the 500SEC and 500SEL sedans. The 5.0-liter coupe was actually 10 pounds lighter than the 380SEC and incorporated an updated rear axle with a torque-compensating device to minimize squat and dive. Interestingly, this also resulted in a shorter wheelbase by a scant 0.2 inches. Updates for 1984 also included an antitheft system and automatically heated front seats. A driver side airbag was optional.

The 5.6-liter V-8 was introduced in 1986. With a longer stroke and different cam design, the power was increased to 238 brake horsepower at 4,800 rpm, which was a 29 percent increase. Other upgrades included a new ignition system and Bosch KE-Jetronic fuel injection.

Throughout production, the four-speed automatic was the only transmission available in the American marketplace. Normally these transmissions start in second gear, but first can be engaged by a quicker throttle application.

The front suspension had unequal length A-arms with coil springs, tube shocks, and an anti-roll bar up front. In the rear were semi-trailing arms, coil springs, tube shocks, and an anti-roll bar. The 560SEC had self-leveling hydropnuematic shock absorbers. The brakes were four-wheel discs that were vented in front and solid in the rear with ABS.

Interior appointments of the W126 SEC are luxurious. Buyers had their choice of either velour or leather upholstery at no additional cost. The front seat design for the coupes offers greater lateral support, which was more in line with the nature of a coupe.

The fully automatic climate control system means you can set a predetermined temperature level and the system will maintain the setting. Electrically adjustable front seats and a telescoping steering column have two programmable memory settings. Controls for the seats are the familiar Mercedes switches that simulate the seat cushion, back, and headrest, which are located in the forward area of the door panel. The front seats have vacuum latches that lock the seatbacks when the engine is started. Burl wood inlays in the dash and door panels complement an electric sunroof, cruise control, power windows, and AM/FM stereo.

The lack of a B-pillar gave the coupe an airy, open feel, but it was a challenge to the design teams to determine where to mount the shoulder belts for the front seat occupants. Their solution was a motorized arm that extends out from the top of the rear quarter window opening and positions the seatbelt just over the outboard shoulder of the driver and passenger. If 30 seconds passes without the seatbelt being buckled, the arm retracts back into the quarter panel. This was the first use of a design that also appeared in the W124 coupe and convertibles.

Supplemental Restraint Systems (airbags) were not available on the 380SEC, but were optional on the 500SEC. By the time the 560SEC arrived, driver side airbags were standard equipment, and the passenger side airbag became standard in 1989.

Production ended in late 1991 and a replacement, the W140 chassis coupe appeared in late 1992. Overall, low production numbers mean a short supply of the W126 coupes. Solid S-class reliability and room for four adults in comfort are distinct advantages. They are heavy cars and fuel economy could be a disadvantage. The 3.8-liter engine had

problems with chain tensioners, so be sure to check maintenance records to confirm this has been fixed.

Watch for gray-market imports, especially of the 500SEC, to make sure everything is taken care of according to U.S. standards. You may also find cars with aftermarket suspensions and wheels. Be sure any of these changes from stock are modifications you can live with. The 500SEC and 560SEC are probably the better buys, primarily for their more powerful engines and the availability of safety items such as ABS and airbags.

The manufacturers' stickers located in the driver-side doorjamb contain a great deal of information. In the upper left corner of the VIN plate is the build date—07/82. The vehicle weights are in the center and top right. The VIN should match the A-pillar plate and the VIN stamped on the firewall. Model type 126C confirms this is a W126 coupe.

The chassis number is stamped on the firewall behind the engine. Compare this to the VIN sticker in the driver's doorjamb and the one attached to the driver-side A-pillar. They should all match. The first six numbers of these VINs match the chassis type designation, 126043. Later cars used a different numbering system as required by the U.S. DOT.

Early SECs, like this 1982 model, will have an interior VIN plate attached to the A-pillar. Later-model cars will have it at the forward, left corner of the dashboard. Either way, the VIN should match the manufacturers' VIN plate in the driver's doorjamb and the one stamped on the firewall.

There is plenty of leg- and headroom for two adults in the rear seats. A first aid kit is stored under the package tray behind the right rear seat. The center armrest adds another touch of individuality to the rear seats. The quarter windows do not disappear completely and leave just the upper corner visible. Seatbelt extenders for the front-seat occupants deliver shoulder belts when the engine is started.

Rating Chart
W126 380SEC/500SEC/560SEC Coupes,
1982–1991

Model	Comfort/Amenities	Reliability	Collectibility	Parts/Service Availability	Est. Annual Repair Costs
380SEC	★★★⯨	★★★★	★★⯨	★★★⯨	★★★⯨
500SEC	★★★★	★★★★	★★⯨	★★★⯨	★★★⯨
560SEC	★★★★	★★★★	★★⯨	★★★⯨	★★★⯨

Common Parts List: W126 380SEC, 1982–1983

Engine:

Oil filter	$8.00
Fuel filter	$42.50
Fuel pump(s)	$266.00
Starter	$177.00 (rebuilt)
Alternator	$389.00 (rebuilt)
Radiator	$486.00
Fan clutch	$460.00
Water pump	$248.00

Body:

Front bumper	$1,516.00
Hood	$2,530.00
Left front fender	$418.00
Right rear quarter panel	$680.00
Rear bumper	$875.00
Windshield	$795.00
Headlight assembly	$10.00
Taillight lens	$244.00

Exhaust:

Catalytic converter (aftermarket)	$450.48
Center muffler	$360.00
Rear muffler	$410.00
Oxygen sensor	$101.00

Chassis:

Brake master	$250.00
Front rotor	$112.00 each
Front pads (set)	$117.00
Front shocks	$130.00 each
Rear shocks:	
Std & H.D.	$140.00 each
Self-leveling	$810.00 each

Technical Specifications: W126 380SEC, 1982–1983

Engine:

Type	SOHC, 90-degree V-8, aluminum block
Displacement cc/ci	3,839/234.3
Compression ratio	8.3:1
Bhp @ rpm	155 @ 4,750
Torque ft-lb @ rpm	196 @ 2,750
Injection type	Bosch K-Jetronic
Fuel requirement	Unleaded, 91 octane

Chassis/drivetrain:

Transmission	Four-speed automatic
Steering	recirculating ball, power-assisted
Front suspension	Unequal-length A-arms, coil springs, tube shocks, anti-roll bar
Rear suspension	Semi-trailing arms, coil springs, tube shocks, anti-roll bar
Differential	2.47:1

General:

Wheelbase	112.2
Weight	3,750
Wheels	14x6.5J, alloy
Tires	205/70HR-14
Brake system:	Four-wheel disc, vacuum-assisted
Front	11.3-inch vented discs
Rear	11.0-inch vented discs
0–60 mph	9.8 sec
Maximum speed mph	115
Fuel economy:	city/hwy
EPA estimated mpg	17/22

Common Parts List: W126 500SEC, 1982–1983

Engine:

Oil filter	$8.00
Fuel filter	$42.50
Fuel pump(s)	$266.00
Starter	$177.00 (rebuilt)
Alternator	$389.00 (rebuilt)
Radiator	$486.00
Fan clutch	$460.00
Water pump	$248.00

Body:

Front bumper	$1,516.00
Hood	$2,530.00
Left front fender	$418.00
Right rear quarter panel	$680.00
Rear bumper	$875.00
Windshield	$795.00
Headlight assembly:	$10.00
Headlight bulb	$2.50
Taillight lens	$244.00

Exhaust:

Catalytic converter (aftermarket)	$450.48
Center muffler	$360.00
Rear muffler	$410.00
Oxygen sensor	$90.00

Chassis:

Brake master	$250.00
Front rotor	$112.00 each
Front pads (set)	$117.00
Front shocks	$130.00 each
Rear shocks:	
Std & H.D.	$140.00 each
Self-leveling	$810.00 each

Common Parts List: W126 560SEC, 1982–1983

Engine:

Oil filter	$8.00
Fuel filter	$42.50
Fuel pump(s)	$252.50
Starter	$177.00 (rebuilt)
Alternator	$389.00 (rebuilt)
Radiator	$486.00
Fan clutch	$460.00
Water pump	$280.00

Body:

Front bumper	$1,516.00
Hood	$2,530.00
Left front fender	$418.00
Right rear quarter panel	$680.00
Rear bumper	$875.00
Windshield	$795.00
Headlight	$595.00
Taillight lens	$244.00

Exhaust:

Catalytic converter (including front pipe)	$2,370.00
Rear muffler	$855.00
Oxygen sensor	$118.00

Chassis:

Brake master	$212.00
Front rotor	$75.00 each
Front pads (set)	$48.00
Front shocks	$130.00 each
Rear shocks:	
Std & H.D.	$140.00 each
Self-leveling	$324.00 each

Technical Specifications: W126 500SEC, 1984–1985

Engine:

Type	SOHC 90-degree V-8, aluminum block
Displacement cc/ci	4,973/303
Compression ratio	8.0:1
Bhp @ rpm	184 @ 4,500
Torque ft-lb @ rpm	247 @ 2,000
Injection type	Bosch K-Jetronic
Fuel requirement	Unleaded, 91 octane

Chassis/drivetrain:

Transmission	Four-speed automatic
Steering	Recirculating ball, power-assisted
Front suspension	Unequal-length A-arms, coil springs, tube shocks, anti-roll bar
Rear suspension	Semi-trailing arms, coil springs, tube shocks, anti-roll bar
Differential	2.47:1

General:

Wheelbase	112.2
Weight	3,655
Wheels	14x6.5J, forged alloy
Tires	205/70HR-14
Brake system:	Four-wheel disc, vacuum-assisted
Front	11.3-inch vented discs
Rear	11.0-inch vented discs
0–60 mph	9.0 sec
Maximum speed mph	125 (est.)
Fuel economy:	city/hwy
EPA estimated mpg	17/22

Technical Specifications: W126 560SEC, 1986–1991

Engine:

Type	SOHC 90-degree V-8, aluminum block
Displacement cc/ci	5,547/339
Compression ratio	9.0:1
Bhp @ rpm	238 @ 4,800
Torque ft-lb @ rpm	287 @ 3,500
Injection type	Bosch KE-Jetronic
Fuel requirement	Unleaded, 91 octane

Chassis/drivetrain:

Transmission	Four-speed automatic
Steering	Recirculating ball, power-assisted
Front suspension	Unequal-length A-arms, coil springs, tube shocks, anti-roll bar
Rear suspension	Semi-trailing arms, coil springs, tube shocks, anti-roll bar
Differential	2.47:1

General:

Wheelbase	112.2
Weight	3,960
Wheels	14x6.5J, forged alloy
Tires	205/70HR-14
Brake system:	Four-wheel disc, vacuum-assisted, ABS
Front	11.8-inch vented discs
Rear	11.0-inch vented discs
0–60 mph	8.0 sec
Maximum speed mph	140 (est.)
Fuel economy:	city/hwy
EPA estimated mpg	13/17

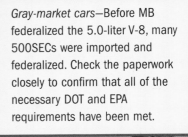

Gray-market cars—Before MB federalized the 5.0-liter V-8, many 500SECs were imported and federalized. Check the paperwork closely to confirm that all of the necessary DOT and EPA requirements have been met.

Plastic tank radiators—Check these for evidence of leaking. Over time, plastic becomes brittle and hose necks can break off. Later style Behr radiators have reinforced hose necks.

Timing chains (3.8-liter)—Have a mechanic pull a valve cover and check for single- or double-row chains in 1982 and 1983 models. The single-row chains tend to wear and stretch. If stretched, the chain can jump a tooth and result in valve-to-piston contact. The 1984 and on models used double-row chains.

O. E. Becker Grand Prix radios—Many of the original Becker radios had problems. While having an original radio is nice, an aftermarket radio might actually be a better deal.

Trunk—A deteriorated trunk seal can let water seep into trunk. Lift mats to look for water damage or rust.

Power windows—Confirm that the front and rear windows function properly.

HVAC systems—The climate control systems are complex. Make sure the system functions and that all of the various settings for airflow work properly. Correcting malfunctions can get expensive.

Dashboard—The upper surface of the dash is constantly exposed to sunlight. Look for evidence of the dash drying out and cracking.

Chapter 12

W140 Coupes: 1993 –1999 500SEC/S500/CL500/ 600SEC/S600/CL600

Basic History

Development of the W126 coupe replacement actually began prior to 1985. Initially targeted for release in 1987, the engineering team found additional development requirements that delayed the release of the W140 S-class coupes until 1992.

The coupe is an all-new design. The wheelbase is 3.8 inches shorter than the S-class short-wheelbase sedan and is 45 pounds lighter. Sharing the engines, suspension, and brakes of the new S-class, the 500SEC and 600SEC were the flagship models of the Mercedes-Benz lineup. They were equipped with the latest technical advances, and there were few items remaining on the options list. Even metallic paint was available at no additional cost.

The front and rear glass is bonded to the body shell, which added structural rigidity to the body. The side windows are double paned to insulate against noise and temperature. When the door handle is pulled, the side window drops down slightly to easily open the door. When the door is closed, the window raises back up against the rubber door seal.

The doors and trunk have a closing assist feature that automatically completes the closing of both. Distance sensors are in both bumpers and sound an audible warning when the driver is close to a fixed object. A matching periscope at the upper corner of each rear fender pops up when reverse is selected.

During the W140s production run, several updates were made to the cars. The V-8-powered coupes received the Xenon High Intensity Discharge (HID) lights and an integrated garage door opener in 1997.

The Electronic Brake Force Distribution (EBF) integrated with ABS, and the Parktronic electronic parking system and a rain sensor to automatically adjust the wiper delay were added as standard equipment in 1998. Driver and passenger airbags also became standard equipment that year. In addition, both the S500 and S600 received CFC-free climate control systems and BabySmart, a system that automatically deactivates the passenger side airbag when a compatible child seat is properly installed.

The 5.0-liter DOHC 32-valve all-alloy V-8 produced 315 brake horsepower at 5,600 rpm and 347 foot-pounds of torque at 3,900 rpm and is sufficient to propel the coupes to 60 miles per hour in 7.2 seconds. The 390 brake horsepower all-alloy DOHC four-valve per cylinder V-12 pushes the 5,000-plus pound coupe to 60 miles per hour in 6.6 seconds. The chain-driven intake camshafts offer variable valve timing to improve midrange torque and higher rpm power, smooth low speed idle, and reduce emissions.

Delivering the power to the rear wheels, a four-speed electronically controlled transmission was standard through 1995. In 1996, a driver-adaptive, electronically controlled five-speed automatic replaced the earlier gearbox.

Independent suspension is standard Mercedes-Benz fare. Double wishbones with separate gas-charged shocks, coil springs, and stabilizer bar are used in the front suspension. The rear suspension is Mercedes-Benz's five-arm multilink system that incorporates anti-lift, anti-squat, and alignment control. Coil springs, stabilizer bar, and self-leveling shocks complete the rear suspension. Road feel is improved and low-speed parking efforts are made easier by the speed-sensitive, power-assisted, and hydraulically damped recirculating ball steering.

The braking system is dual-circuit, hydraulically power-assisted four-wheel vented disc brakes. ABS and front-to-rear brake force proportioning are standard. Brake Assist senses a panic-stop and reduces the time from touching the brake pedal to the application of the brakes that helps shorten braking distances.

The heated, individual front bucket seats have three memory settings that are also coordinated with the steering wheel position and mirror settings. Front and side airbags protect occupants, and the now-familiar motorized arms extend out from the B-pillars to deliver the three-point shoulder belt to driver and passenger.

The dash is the only interior item that is shared with the sedans. The instrument cluster houses an electronic analog speedometer, tachometer, and a combined gauge for fuel level, coolant temperature, oil pressure, and fuel economy readout. Additionally, there is an electronic digital odometer, a trip meter, quartz clock, and outside temperature indicator. Along the bottom row of the cluster are warning lights for various systems. The Mercedes-Benz Flexible Service System (FSS) monitors and displays distance to next oil change or service and is based on actual driving conditions.

The center console features controls for the dual climate-control systems, electrostatic air filtration, a defeat switch for the traction-control system, a button to raise or lower the rear seat headrests, and a button to control the rear window sunshade.

The option list was short. Literally everything was standard equipment on the V-12 cars. Options for the V-8-powered cars included onboard phone, compact disc-changer and variable suspension damping, Electronic Stability Program (ESP), Adaptive Damping System (ADS) multicontour front seats, a power glass sunroof, and an electric rear window sunshade. Metallic paints were a no-charge option.

In 1994, Mercedes re-aligned all their model designations and swapped the numbers and letters. The W140 coupes were renamed from the 500SEC/600SEC to the S500 and S600 coupes. If this wasn't confusing enough, the names were changed again in 1998 to the CL500 and CL600. The cars themselves did not change, only the model names.

Production of the W140 S-class ended in 1999, and the new W215-based CL500 and CL600 coupes came to market in model year 2000. Extravagant and opulent, the flowing design has a grace about it that befits a car of this category. These big coupes were never imported in large numbers, and 19 CL500 and 15 CL600s were imported in 1991, its final year. Will they be coveted and collected like the 1970s 280SE coupes in 30 years? Their small overall numbers may mean they could be.

The fit and finish for these models are first-rate. Performance is exceptional for a car of this size and heft. They offer comfortable room for four adults and enough trunk space to carry plenty of luggage. If one of these suits your purposes, the V-12 cars are probably the better long-term collectible.

The ribbed taillight lens design helps keep dirt from collecting. To the left of the key-operated trunk lock is an infrared sensor for the remote locking system. At the top corner of both rear fenders are antenna-like posts that extend when reverse is selected and aid the driver when backing up.

The manufacturers' stickers in driver-side doorjamb provide SRS airbag replacement dates, VIN, vehicle capacity, and weights. The VIN should match the plate attached to the dashboard. Missing stickers or overspray are likely indications of repairs.

The rear seats are accommodating, and the switches between the seats are for rear-seat adjustments. The seatbelt extenders for front-seat occupants deliver shoulder belts when the engine is started.

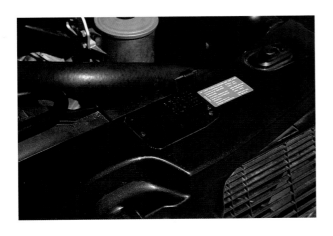

Although it is difficult to see in this photo, the chassis plate is attached to the radiator core support. The second line is the chassis type designation. The V-8 coupes should be type 140070, and V-12 coupes should be 140076.

Rating Chart
W140 500S/S500/CL500/600S/S600/CL600
Coupes, 1993–1999

Model	Comfort/Amenities	Reliability	Collectibility	Parts/Service Availability	Est. Annual Repair Costs
500S/S500/CL500	★★★★	★★★⌡	★★⌡	★★★⌡	★★★⌡
600S/S600/CL600	★★★★	★★★⌡	★★⌡	★★★⌡	★★★⌡

Common Parts List: W140 500SEC/ S500/CL500, 1993–1999

Engine:
Oil filter	$13.00
Fuel filter	$45.00
Fuel pump(s) (two per car)	$252.00 each
Starter	$254.50 (rebuilt)
Alternator:	$449.00 (rebuilt)
150 amp	$627.00 (rebuilt)
Radiator	$555.00
Fan clutch	$480.00
Water pump	$418.00

Body:
Front bumper	$891.70
Hood	$1,480.00
Left front fender	$404.00
Right rear quarter panel	$1,140.00
Rear bumper	$1,100.00
Windshield	$735.00
Headlight assembly:	$715.00
Gas-discharge Xenon	$1,600.00
Taillight lens:	
to 1996	$190.00
from 1997	$216.00

Exhaust:
Catalytic converter (including front pipe)	$2,610.00
Muffler	$808.50
Oxygen sensor	$129.00

Chassis:
Brake master	$1,450.00
Front rotor	$90.00 each
Front pads (set)	$89.00
Front shocks (not w/ADS)	$187.00 each
Rear shocks:	
Standard	$202.00 each
Self-leveling (not w/ADS)	$640.00 each

Technical Specifications: W140 500SEC/S500/ CL500, 1993–1999

Engine:
Type	DOHC 32-valve V-8, alloy block and heads
Displacement cc/ci	4,973/303
Compression ratio	10.0:1
Bhp @ rpm	315 @ 5,600
Torque ft-lb @ rpm	347 @ 3,900
Injection type	ME 1.0 fully electronic w/anti-knock and electronic throttle
Fuel requirement	Premium, 91 octane

Chassis/drivetrain:
Transmission:	
1991–1995	Four-speed automatic
1996–on	Five-speed automatic
Steering	Recirculating ball w/speed sensitive power-assist
Front suspension	Independent double wishbone, coil springs, gas-pressure shocks, anti-roll bar, anti-dive geometry
Rear suspension	Five-link w/geometry for anti-lift, anti-squat, and alignment control, anti-roll bar, hypopneumatic shock absorbers and coil springs. Automatic rear-axle level control
Differential	2.65:1

General:
Wheelbase	115.9
Weight	4,695
Wheels	16x7.5J
Tires	235/60R-16
Brake system:	Four-wheel disc, power-assisted, ABS, Brake Assist
Front	12.6-in vented discs
Rear	11.8-in vented discs
0–60 mph	7.2 sec
Maximum speed mph	155 (electronically limited)
Fuel economy:	city/hwy
EPA estimated mpg	13/15

Common Parts List: W140 600SEC/S600/CL600, 1993–1999

Engine:

Oil filter	$21.50
Fuel filter	$45.00
Fuel pump(s):	
600SEC/S600 (two per car)	$252.00 each
CL600	$197.00
Starter	$365.20 (rebuilt)
Alternator	$471.90 (rebuilt)
Radiator	$478.00
Fan clutch	$575.00
Water pump	$500.00

Body:

Front bumper	$891.00
Hood	$1,480.00
Left front fender	$404.00
Right rear quarter panel	$1,140.00
Rear bumper	$1,100.00
Windshield	$735.00

Headlight assembly:	
to 1996	$715.00
from 1997 (gas-discharge Xenon)	$1,600.00
Taillight lens:	
to 1996	$190.00
from 1997	$216.00

Exhaust:

Catalytic converter (including front pipe):	
Left	$1,440.00
Right	$1,570.00
Muffler (including tailpipe)	$675.00
Oxygen sensor (two per car)	$129.00 each

Chassis:

Brake master	$1,450.00
Front rotor	$90.00 each
Front pads (set)	$89.00
Front shocks (not w/ADS)	$187.00 each
Rear shocks:	$202.00 each
Self-leveling (not w/ADS)	$640.00 each

Technical Specifications: W140 600SEC/S600/CL600, 1993–1999

Engine:

Type	DOHC 48-valve V-12, alloy block and heads
Displacement cc/ci	5,987/365
Compression ratio	10.0:1
Bhp @ rpm	389 @ 5,200
Torque ft-lb @ rpm	420 @ 3,800
Injection type	ME 1.0 fully electronic w/anti-knock and electronic throttle
Fuel requirement	Premium, 91 octane

Chassis/drivetrain:

Transmission:	
1992–1995	Four-speed automatic
1996–on	Five-speed automatic
Steering	Recirculating ball w/speed sensitive power-assist
Front suspension	independent double wishbone, coil springs, gas-pressure shocks, anti-roll bar, anti-dive geometry
Rear suspension	Five-link w/geometry for anti-lift, anti-squat and alignment control, anti-roll bar, hypopneumatic shock absorbers and coil springs. Automatic rear-axle level control
Differential	2.65:1

General:

Wheelbase	115.9
Weight	5,105 pounds
Wheels:	
1996	16x7.5J fr/16x8.0 rear
1997–on	16x7.5J
Tires	235/60R-16
Brake system:	Four-wheel disc, power-assisted, ABS, Brake Assist
Front	12.6-in vented discs
Rear	11.8-in vented discs
0–60 mph	6.3 sec
Maximum speed mph	155 (electronically limited)
Fuel economy:	city/hwy
EPA estimated mpg	15/19

All Models:

Window regulators—Operate windows through their full range several times. Listen for any unusual noises from the window mechanisms. There have been many reports of failed window regulators, usually in the down position during the rainy season.

Motor mounts—Let the car idle in gear. Listen and feel for more than a usual amount of vibration from the car. It could be a symptom of motor mounts that have failed. They are filled with hydraulic fluid, and over time they will go bad. Replacement mounts result in a return of a smooth idle. Have these checked during the prepurchase inspection.

A/C evaporator—Check for a musty or sweet smell when the A/C system is on. Repairing the evaporator requires removing the dashboard. Figure a minimum of 8 to 12 hours of labor plus parts. There are many diaphragms and vacuum lines in there, and doing the job right takes time. While you are in there, it might be good to have the regulator flaps replaced. It saves going back in a second time.

Fuel-injection wiring harnesses—Engine heat causes insulation to prematurely dry out, crack, and disintegrate. This can begin at the 50,000- to 60,000-mile mark, and by 100,000 miles, it is usually severe. Be mindful of these because bad insulation may result in wires shorting and can damage the engine's computers. Harnesses are between $350 to $800, depending on car. Leave this repair to a qualified mechanic.

Power steering pumps—Check the pump for evidence of leaks. The best way to check is from underneath. Look for moisture in, around, and on the pump. Four different pumps were used and can cost more than $1,200. Kits are available to reseal the pumps, and figure six to eight hours of labor plus parts. On cars with self-leveling suspensions, the power steering pump provides pressure for both systems, and the repairs take longer and cost even more.

500S/S500/CL500

Valve cover gaskets—Look for leaking valve cover gaskets. It is common and fairly easy to replace.

Head gaskets—Gaskets are good for up to 100,000 miles. At that point, begin watching for signs of head gaskets that need to be replaced.

Fan belt tensioners—Tensioners should be checked at regular intervals. Check service receipts to see if and when this may have been done. If it hasn't, have them replaced as soon as it is practical.

Door and trunk closing-assist feature—Confirm this feature works because it seems to be a common failure item.

Engine—Raise the hood and listen for tapping or ticking from the engine's top end. This may indicate the plastic oil supply tubes for rockers that have become dislodged. Have these checked as soon as it is practical. It is not that hard to fix and you are saving money by replacing them as soon as you can. Fix leaky valve cover gaskets at same time.

Chapter 13

W215 CL500/ CL55 AMG/CL600: 2000–on
Basic History

New for 2000, the W215 chassis CL500 was the last car designed under the tutelage of Bruno Sacco prior to his retirement. It is a graceful design and is a technological tour-de-force that features composite materials and state-of-the-art electronics.

The new CL is 2.8 inches shorter, 2.2 inches narrower, and 2.3 inches lower than the coupe it replaced. The wheelbase is shorter by 2.3 inches, but you don't notice it from the inside because the interior dimensions are actually bigger than the W140 chassis coupe.

In a departure from the past, this full-size coupe is not based on the S-class sedan. It does share engines with the sedan, but the chassis itself is unique to the CL coupes.

Combining hybrid composite construction technologies, an aluminum sheet forms the roof skin, door skins, hood, and rear fenders. The inner doorframes are magnesium and the bumpers, front fenders, and trunk lid are high impact plastic panels. All together, the W215 body shell has 58 percent greater torsional strength than its predecessor. The drag coefficient is 0.28, which is the lowest on record for a luxury coupe. The attention to detail and small items such as the plastic under tray beneath the engine and passenger compartment, small spoilers ahead of each rear wheel, and a small deck lid spoiler help eliminate drag.

The navigation system and cellular phone antennas are imbedded in the trunk lid. The door hinges are multilink, and the doors move outward as they pivot to prevent the leading edge of the doors from interfering with the front fenders and for easy entry and exit to the car.

The windshield has integrated ports for electronic devices. One is in the upper portion for toll booth pass devices, and a lower one is for radar detectors. The headlights are Bi-Xenon HID lights.

Aimed at a clientele with incomes in the mid-six figure range, the W215 comes with an array of electronic features. Some were brought over from the S-class sedan, and some are unique to these coupes. The COMAND system administers the audio, navigation, telephone, and environmental systems. Driver aids include ABS, Electronic Brake Force Distribution, ESP yaw control, and an onboard computer networks that administers traction control.

Active Body Control (ABC) is only available on these coupes and isn't shared with any of the other platforms. Similar to an active suspension system, ABC can be switched between comfort and sport modes. The system controls body roll during cornering, braking, and acceleration. Traditional anti-sway bars are not used. Sensors at each corner monitor and compare what is occurring and sends signals to microprocessors that send signals to accumulators at each wheel that feed pressurized hydraulic oil to or from the shocks and stiffen or soften the ride characteristics on the fly.

While the above description is simplified, the mechanics of the system are incredibly complex and effective. At low speed, the body can be raised for ground clearance in parking lots. At speeds above 87 miles per hour, the body is automatically lowered 0.4 inches for lessened wind resistance and better fuel economy.

Keyless Go, a feature of current models, is a pass-card system that locks and unlocks the doors with a touch of a sensor. You can also start the engine by putting a foot on the brake pedal and placing a finger on a touch-sensitive pad atop the shift lever. You do need to have the pass card on your person to do this. Touching the pad can also turn off the engine.

The optional TeleAid system uses the onboard GPS and a dedicated cellular link to provide 24/7 contact with Mercedes-Benz for roadside assistance and information.

Power for the W215 comes through a trio of engine choices. Based on a modular design, this family of engines is available in V-6, V-8, and V-12 configurations. Both the V-8s used in the CL500 and CL55 AMG and the V-12 used in the CL600 are all alloy blocks and heads with chain-driven single overhead cams, three-valves per cylinder (two intake and one exhaust valve), and twin plugs per cylinder. The intake manifold uses variable length runners for improved throttle response at low rpms and better power at higher rpms.

Engines for the CL55 AMG are hand assembled by the staff at AMG and each engine has a signed plaque attached to the intake plenum. In 2003, the AMG model received a belt-driven supercharger, twin-intercoolers, and sequential fuel injection. Power was raised from 355 brake horsepower at 5,500 revs to 493 brake horsepower at 6,100 revs. Torque jumped from 391 to 516 foot-pounds.

The CL600's 60-degree V-12 features an automatic cylinder cutout. When it runs below 3,000 rpm and at throttle positions of one-half or less, one bank of cylinders is electronically disabled by the engine management computer. Fuel mileage gains are estimated at up to 20 percent over normal operation on all 12 cylinders.

Twin exhaust-driven turbochargers, twin intercoolers and sequential fuel injection were new for the 2003 CL600. It cranked out 590 foot-pounds of torque from 1,800 to 3,500 rpm. Horsepower rose from 362 brake horsepower at 5,500 rpm to 493 brake horsepower at 5,000. Zero-to-60–mile per hour times dropped from 5.9 seconds to 4.6 seconds. Top speed for all three of the CL coupes is electronically limited to 155 miles per hour.

Transmitting all of this power is a five-speed, electronically controlled TouchShift automatic with overdrive. Gear selections are done by a sideways flick of the shift lever. The CL55 models received AMG's SpeedShift with upshifts that are up to 35 percent quicker than standard. Buttons on the back of the steering wheel allow the driver to change gears without taking a hand off the steering wheel.

Bringing all of this to a stop are four-wheel disc brakes. Befitting of cars of this potential, the brake systems are also quite special. The CL500 and CL600 use cross-drilled and ventilated rotors on the front and rear. Brembo four-piston calipers are up front, and the rear has two-piston calipers. The CL55 AMG brakes for 2003 were upgraded to AMG eight-piston calipers in front with AMG four-piston calipers in the rear. All four corners receive cross-drilled and ventilated rotors.

Standard are ABS brakes; the Electronic Brake Force Distribution (EBF), which is used to distribute braking forces more evenly; and Brake Assist. Brake Assist detects emergency braking by sensing the speed the driver presses the brake pedal and immediately applies maximum available power-assist boost.

Electronic tire pressure sensors are located in each tire's valve stem and transmit signals to receivers located in each wheelwell, notifying the driver if tire pressures have dropped. A "Check Tire Pressure" light in the instrument panel will illuminate and indicate which tire(s) pressure has dropped below a driver-programmed setting.

In the interior, leather is everywhere. The CL600s have Alcantara on the door pillars and headliner. Two-tone leather could also be ordered, and owners could choose between chestnut or burled walnut inlays for the dash, center console, steering wheel, shift knob, and gate.

The motorized extender arms of prior coupes have been replaced by seatbelts that are integrated with the front seats. The front seats have internal fans to help cool backsides and are also heated.

Instrumentation includes analog speedometer, tachometer, fuel, and coolant. An alphanumeric message center displays odometer readings, trip computer, radio station, next navigation instruction, and other messages. The Flexible Service System (FSS) monitors driving style and displays the distance remaining to the next regular maintenance service.

While the list of standard equipment covered much of what anyone would want, there were a couple of items that could be included. A Sport Package with larger wheels and tires, and Parktronic, a series of sensors that send an audible tone when getting too close to objects while backing up, were both available as options.

Distronic cruise control, a system that "looks ahead" for traffic and automatically slows the coupe down to a matching speed and maintains a preset distance from the car in front, is available on the CL600.

The W215s are delightful, sensuous-looking coupes that embody state-of-the-art construction technology and electronics. These could be both the CL coupe's strongest assets, as well as a future weakness. The electronics in today's cars are pretty reliable and the first owners are covered by the factory warranty. Subsequent owners will not have the warranty, and when an electronic module fails and needs replacement, the repair bills will be breathtakingly expensive. The big coupes will always have a higher collectibility factor than sedans. In the long term, the question will always be, will today's cars have the collectible status of the early cars? Time will tell.

There is a choice of chestnut or burled walnut inlays and two-tone leather for the interior. The leather cover on the top dash surface needs to be treated regularly to keep it from drying out and cracking. The cupholder comes up from the center console, between the storage compartment and shift quadrant. Spilled liquid can infiltrate the shifter and cause electrical problems.

The trunk is generous and well appointed. The spare tire and jack are stored underneath the carpeted mat.

These coupes are among the last designs under the guidance of Bruno Sacco. They will still look good many years from now.

There is plenty of room for two adults in this coupe. The rear headrests can be raised or lowered electrically. The center armrest contains a first aid kit. Two round emblems in the lower corners of the seats are the child seat latch-points.

The 5.5-liter engines in AMG cars are hand assembled. Look for any signs of fluid leaks and accident damage repairs.

The V-8 Kompressor script behind the front wheel indicates this is the CL55 AMG version of the coupe. Use of composite and lightweight materials helps keep the weight down. Check the fit and finish for evidence of accident damage repairs.

The panel fit should be even and consistent. The round objects in the front bumper are Parktronic sensors to warn when the driver is close to stationary objects.

The trunk offers plenty of room. The first aid kit at right can be stowed in the rear-seat center armrest. The full-size spare tire has a tidy storage tray in the center for tools and spare fuses. The jack is located on the left side.

Parktronic sensors are also located in the rear bumper to warn the driver of stationary objects. The left taillight has an integrated rear fog light.

The center armrest storage is impressive. The cupholder can accommodate two drinks, but be careful not to spill liquid into an electronic shifter. The COMAND system occupies a spot in the center of the dash. Multifunction steering wheel buttons control dash displays, radio, and COMAND functions.

Manufacturers' stickers are located in the driver-side door-jamb. The VIN should match the plate located in the lower left front corner of the dashboard. Missing stickers or overspray may be indications of accident damage repairs.

The glorious V-12 engine features an automatic cylinder cut-out that disables one bank of cylinders during low-throttle situations to increase gas mileage by up to 20 percent. The 2003 models received twin turbochargers and intercoolers.

The rear seats are luxurious and comfortable. Side-impact airbags and head-protection curtains protect rear-seat passengers. The center armrest folds down and has an integrated storage compartment. Two round symbols in the lower corners of the rear seats indicate child seat latching points.

Common Parts List: W215 CL500, 2000–on

Engine:

Oil filter	$18.50
Fuel filter	$109.00
Fuel pump(s)	$340.00
Starter	$253.75 (rebuilt)
Alternator	$627.00 (rebuilt)
Electric cooling fan	$740.00
Water pump	$206.00
Radiator	$545.00

Body:

Front bumper	$745.00
Hood	$1,440.00
Left front fender	$505.00
Right rear quarter panel	$1,170.00
Rear bumper	$1,460.00
Windshield	$835.00
Headlight assembly	$1,430.00
Taillight lens	$150.00

Exhaust:

Catalytic converter (with converter):	
Left:	
Front	$1,260.00
Rear	$580.00
Muffler:	
Left	$580.00
Right	$350.00
Oxygen sensor (two per car, before converter)	
Left	$204.00
Right	$204.00

Chassis:

Vacuum brake booster:	$294.00
Brake fluid reservoir	$91.00
Front rotor	$117.00 each
Front pads (set)	$122.00
Front shocks (w/four-link)	$1,470.00 each
Rear shocks:	
w/active suspension:	
Left	$1,400.00
Right	$1,470.00
w/o active suspension	$980.00 each

Rating Chart
W215 CL500/CL55 AMG/CL600, 2000–on

Model	Comfort/Amenities	Reliability	Collectibility	Parts/Service Availability	Est. Annual Repair Costs
CL500	★★★★	★★★★	★★★⨼	★★★⨼	★★★⨼
CL55 AMG	★★★★	★★★★	★★★⨼	★★★⨼	★★★⨼
CL600	★★★★	★★★★	★★★⨼	★★★⨼	★★★⨼

Common Parts List:
W215 CL55 AMG, 2002–2003

Engine:

Oil filter	$18.50
Fuel filter	$109.00
Fuel pump(s)	$340.00
Starter	$253.75 (rebuilt)
Alternator	$627.00 (rebuilt)
Electric cooling fan	$740.00
Water pump	$206.00
Radiator	$545.00

Body:

Front bumper:	
w/sport pkg.:	
2001–2002	$2,920.00
2003–on	$1,460.00
w/o sport pkg.:	
2001–2002	$745.00
2003–on	$615.00
Hood	$1,440.00
Left front fender	$505.00
Right rear quarter panel	$1,170.00
Rear bumper	$1,460.00
Windshield	$835.00
Headlight assembly	$1,430.00
Taillight lens	$150.00

Exhaust:

Catalytic converter (with converter):	
Left:	
Front	$1,260.00
Rear	$580.00
Right	$1,260.00
Muffler:	
Left	$580.00
Right	$350.00
Oxygen sensor (two per car, before converter)	
Left	$204.00
Right	$204.00

Chassis:

Vacuum brake booster:	$294.00
Brake fluid reservoir	$91.00
Front rotor	$117.00 each
Front pads (set)	$122.00

Technical Specifications: W215 CL500, 2000–2004

Engine:

Type	SOHC 90-degree V-8, two intake valves/one exhaust valve per cylinder
Displacement cc/ci	4966/303
Compression ratio	10.0:1
Bhp @ rpm	302 @ 5600
Torque ft-lb @ rpm	339 @ 2700-4250
Injection type	Sequential fuel injection, electronic throttle control
Engine management	ME 2.8 w/phase-shifted twin plugs per cylinder, two coils per cylinder
Fuel requirement	Regular, 91 octane

Chassis/drivetrain:

Transmission	Five-speed electronically controlled automatic w/Touch Shift and driver-adaptive shift logic
Steering	Recirculating ball, hydraulic power-assist
Front suspension	Upper and lower control arms, coil springs, electrohydraulic damping plus gas-charged tube shocks, level control
Rear suspension	Five-link, coil springs, electrohydraulic damping plus gas-charged tube shocks, level control
Differential	2.82:1

General:

Wheelbase	113.6
Weight (pounds)	4,070
Wheels:	17x7.5 alloy
2003 sport pkg.	18x8.5 alloy fr/18x9.0 rear
Tires:	225/55ZR-17
2003 sport pkg.	245/45ZR-18 fr/265/40ZR-18 rear
Brake system:	Hydraulic power-assisted four-wheel discs w/four-channel ABS; Brake Assist system
Front	13.1-inch vented and drilled discs
Rear	11.8-inch vented discs
0–60 mph	6.1 sec
Maximum speed mph	155 (electronically limited)
Fuel economy:	city/hwy
EPA estimated mpg	16/23

Common Parts List:
W215 CL600, 2002–2003

Engine:

Oil filter	$18.50
Fuel filter	$109.00
Fuel pump(s)	$340.00
Starter	$253.75 (rebuilt)
Alternator	$627.00 (rebuilt)
Electric cooling fan:	
Puller	$635.00
Pusher	$408.00
Water pump	$206.00
Radiator	$545.00

Body:

Front bumper	$745.00
Hood	$1,440.00
Left front fender	$505.00
Right rear quarter panel	$1,170.00
Rear bumper	$1,460.00
Windshield	$835.00
Headlight assembly	$1,430.00
Taillight lens	$150.00

Exhaust:

Catalytic converter (with converter):	
Left:	
Front	$710.00
Rear	$1,670.00
Right:	
Front	$745.00
Rear	$1,100.00
Muffler:	
Left	$580.00
Right	$350.00
Oxygen sensor (two per car)	
Front	$159.00
Rear	$159.00

Chassis:

Vacuum brake booster:	$294.00
Brake fluid reservoir	$91.00
Front rotor	$120.00 each
Front pads (set)	$122.00
Front shocks (w/four-link)	$1,470.00 each
Rear shocks:	
w/active suspension	$1,470.00 each
w/o active suspension	$980.00 each

Technical Specifications:
W209 CL55 AMG, 2001–2004

Engine:

Type	SOHC 90-degree V-8, three valves per cylinder
Displacement cc/ci	5,439/331.9
Compression ratio:	
to 2002	10.5:1
2003–on	9.0:1
Bhp @ rpm:	
to 2002	355 @ 5,500
2003–on	493 @ 6,100
Torque ft-lb @ rpm:	
to 2002	391 @ 3,000
2003–on	516 @ 2,650–4,500
Injection type:	
to 2002	Sequential fuel injection, electronic throttle control, two-stage resonance intake manifold
2003–on	Belt-driven supercharger, twin inter coolers, sequential fuel injection, electronic throttle
Engine management	ME 2.8 engine control w/phase-shifted twin sparkplugs per cylinder, two coils per cylinder

Chassis/drivetrain:

Transmission	Five-speed electronically controlled automatic w/Touch Shift and driver-adaptive shift logic
Steering	Recirculating ball, hydraulic power-assist
Front suspension	Upper and lower control arms, coil springs, electrohydraulic damping plus gas-charged tube shocks, level control
Rear suspension	Five-link, coil springs, electrohydraulic damping plus gas-charged tube shocks, level control
Differential	2.82:1

General:

Wheelbase	113.6
Weight:	
to 2002	4,080
2003–on	4,255
Wheels:	
to 2002	18x8.5 fr/18x9.5 rear, Monoblock
2003–on	18x8.5 fr/18x9.0 rear
Tires:	
to 2002	245/45YR-18 fr/275/40YR-18 rear
2003–on	245/45ZR-18 fr/265/40ZR-18 rear
Brake system:	Hydraulic power-assisted four-wheel discs w/four-channel ABS; Brake Assist system
Front:	
to 2002	13.6-inch vented and drilled discs
2003–on	14.17-inch vented, perforated discs
Rear:	
to 2002	12.4-inch vented discs
2003–on	13.0-inch vented, perforated discs
0–60 mph:	
to 2002	5.7 sec
2003–on	4.6 sec
Maximum speed mph	155 (electronically limited)
Fuel economy:	city/hwy
EPA estimated mpg	16/22

Technical Specifications: W215 CL600, 2001–2004

Engine:

Type	SOHC 60 degree V-12, three valves per cylinder
Displacement cc/ci	5,786/353.1
Compression ratio:	
to 2002	10.0:1
2003–on	9.0:1
Bhp @ rpm:	
2002	362 @ 5,500
2003–on	493 @ 5,000
Torque ft-lb @ rpm:	
to 2002	391 @ 4,100
2003–on	590 @ 1,800–3,500
Injection type:	
to 2002	Sequential fuel injection, electronic throttle control, two-stage resonance intake manifold
2003–on	exhaust-driven twin turbochargers, twin intercoolers, sequential fuel injection, electronic throttle
Engine management:	
to 2002	ME 2.7 engine control w/phase-shifted twin sparkplugs per cylinder, two coils per cylinder, Active Cylinder Control
2003–on	phase-shifted twin sparkplugs per cylinder, two coils per cylinder

Chassis/drivetrain:

Transmission	Five-speed electronically controlled automatic w/Touch Shift and driver-adaptive shift logic
Steering	Recirculating ball, hydraulic power-assist
Front suspension	Upper and lower control arms, coil springs, electrohydraulic damping plus gas-charged tube shocks, level control

Rear suspension	Five-link, coil springs, electrohydraulic damping plus gas-charged tube shocks, level control
Differential	2.65:1

General:

Wheelbase	113.6
Weight: (pounds)	
to 2002	4,300
2003–on	4,390
Wheels:	
to 2002	17x7.5 alloy
2003–on	
Tires:	
to 2002	225/55ZR-17
2003–on	
Brake system:	Hydraulic power-assisted four-wheel discs w/four-channel ABS; Brake Assist System
Front:	
to 2002	13.6-inch vented and drilled discs
2003–on	14.2-inch vented, perforated discs
Rear:	
to 2002	12.4-inch vented discs
2003–on	13.0-inch vented, perforated discs
0–60 mph:	
to 2002	5.9 sec
2003–on	4.6 sec
Maximum speed mph	155 (electronically limited)
Fuel economy:	city/hwy
EPA estimated mpg	15/22

Windows—Pull mats and check carpet for dampness due to leaky windows. Frameless windows are notorious for not sealing properly. If there are any problems with the window not sealing tightly, water could leak in.

Climate control blower—There was a recall on the vehicles produced between January and May 2000. The blower motor regulator may develop an electrical short and could cause the surrounding plastic, insulation, or wiring to melt and possibly burn. An updated regulator is installed to resolve a possible problem. Have service technicians check vehicle history to confirm the fix has been done.

Keyless Go—If this feature doesn't work, it could be a weak battery or a module that is going or has gone bad. "Key not recognized" is that message that will appear on the dash display. A dealer can diagnose the system to isolate problem.

Gear shift—Any liquid that is spilled into the center console can find its way into the shift quadrant. If the switch that tells the transmission what gear to be in gets wet and shorts out, it can cause the car to shut down. Be careful when you use the cup holders.

Electrical systems—The electronic systems in these cars are sophisticated and complicated. There are many reports of a variety of problems relating to electrical items malfunctioning or ceasing to function. Be sure to check everything electrical to make sure it works.

Chapter 14

Rare and Collectible MBs 300SL Gullwing and Roadsters: 1954–1963
Basic History

The single Mercedes car that inspired more enthusiasts, the Gullwing coupe, was derived from the successful racing cars of 1952 and 1953. Production of the street cars began in August 1954. The coupes were discontinued in early 1957, and the 300SL roadster was produced from May 1957 to February 1963.

A total of 3,258 cars were built. Of these, 1,400 were coupes and 29 of them were aluminum-bodied and intended for competition use. There were 1,858 roadsters built before production ended. Today, approximately 1,200 coupes are known to have survived, and about 900 of these are in the United States. Approximately 1,458 roadsters are accounted for, and 1,100 of these are in the United States.

With so few of these cars produced, the survivors are well documented and most have been through complete and thorough restorations. Your chances of finding a previously undiscovered or unrestored example are pretty slim.

These cars were expensive when they were new, and they are no less expensive today. It is rare when one comes up for sale, and when that does happen, the prices are well into the six-figure range.

Above right: **The two-piece leather covered luggage was optional, and many owners selected it. The speaker covers are chrome.**
Right: **The dashboard is elegant for its functionality and simplicity. The ventilation slides open or close fresh-air vents. The steering wheel can be unlatched from the steering column and tilts downward, making entry and exiting easier. The radio is located below the dash in the leather-covered fascia.**

Paint—A repaint involves stripping the body, checking for needed bodywork, and making repairs. The cost can easily exceed $40,000.

Frame—The proper way to check for frame damage is to remove the belly pans. Pull the headlight buckets to check for rust, and reach inside of the front fenders to feel for the inner liners. They should be straight. If they aren't, it is an indication of damage and less than correct repairs.

Inspection—Have the car inspected by a specialist. They will know where and what to look for.

Grille—The multipiece, curved-star grille for an early model can cost upward of $10,000.

W121 190SL, 1955–1963

The 190SL is often thought of as the "little brother" of the 300SL, and not without good reason. The 190SL looks similar to the 300SL and capitalized on that model's popularity and was engineered to use as many regular production components as possible to keep the cost down.

Power was provided by an all-new design SOHC four-cylinder that displaced 1,897 cc. Equipped with dual Solex carburetors and producing 105 brake horsepower, the engine has proved to be robust.

The 190SL was first shown at the New York Auto Show in February 1954. Production began in 1955 and ended in February 1963 with 26,000 cars built. Three variations of the car were offered: the basic roadster, a roadster with detachable hardtop, and a closed coupe. Of these, the coupe is the rarest model. Parts are still readily available, including new, factory-replacement sheet metal.

Unless you are a serious do-it-yourselfer, it is probably better to buy a 190SL that is already restored than to buy one and restore it yourself. A nice example will cost about $20,000 to $25,000. A complete restoration will cost at least that much.

The details on this particular car are perfectly done. All cars should be this tidy.

Below: This 1957 300SL Roadster is one of 618 that were built that year. The roadsters use an improved single-pivot swing-axle rear suspension. The design is timeless and looks as good today as it did in 1957.

W180 220S, 1956–1959

Basic History

The 220S, while based on the previous model 220a and retained the W180 chassis designation, featured a larger and more powerful 2,195-cc, twin-carbureted 100 brake horsepower inline six-cylinder that resided under the longer hood.

Visually the 220S can be differentiated from the 220a by the longer hood line from the firewall forward (to accommodate the longer six-cylinder) and the subtle chrome strip that accents the highlight line that runs the length of the front fenders and into the front doors.

Available as a coupe, cabriolet, or sedan, the W180-chassis 220S continued in production through October 1959. Total production of the 220S coupe and cabriolet was 3,429 cars.

The coupes and cabriolets were built on a 5-inch shorter chassis and the floorpan was reinforced for greater strength. The doors are longer and heavier, even though the doorframes are aluminum. The rear bodywork was extended to provide a larger trunk and visually help the overall lines of these cars.

The coupes were not as popular as the cabriolet. Some felt the hardtop did not complement the lines as much. A steel sunroof was a popular option. These coupes and cabriolets were intended as a limited-production vehicle, so the various panels were fitted to each car individually. As a result, these cars were substantially more expensive than the sedan versions.

As the 220S matured, more color combinations were added, horsepower was increased to 106 brake horsepower, and the Hydrak automatic clutch became an option.

The coupe and cabriolet versions make nice cars that are regaining popularity among collectors and enthusiasts.

The W121/190SL 1.9-liter engines are robust and the transmissions are sturdy. A weak point is where the throttle shaft passes through the carburetor body to result in vacuum leaks. Solexes are correct and work fine for show cars. Daily drivers are probably better off with Weber replacements. The battery is a modern-day replica for the original Tar-top battery.

The 190SL chassis serial number is stamped into the cowling directly above the tubular fresh-air vent.

Even the dash in this 190SL resembles the one in the 300SL. Large round dials are easy to read, and the ventilation slides should work easily.

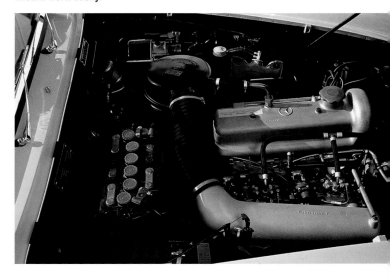

Garage Watch: 190SL

Factory replacement panels—These panels are stamped from the original (old) dies and the replacement pieces may need some detail work to fit properly.

Rust—Check in the battery tray, rear fenders, taillights (above and below; pull and inspect), nose panel, upper front fenders (moisture gets trapped in the headlight buckets; pull and inspect), floorboards, and rockers.

Door joints—
Check the joint
below the door at
the jacking plug
for signs of rust or
incorrect repairs.

Throttle shafts—The throttle shafts wear where they
pass through the body of the carburetors, which
causes vacuum leaks. While Solex carbs were
included in the original equipment, cars that see
regular use may have Weber carbs installed.

W128 220SE, 1958–1960
Basic History

The 220SE coupes and cabriolets share mechanical components with the W128 chassis sedan of the same era. Built on a 5-inch shorter chassis, the floorpans were reinforced for greater strength. The doors are longer and heavier, even though the doorframes are aluminum. The rear bodywork was extended to provide a larger trunk and visually help the overall lines of these cars.

Production ended in October 1959 with a total production run of 1,942 cars. The coupes were not quite as popular as the cabriolet. Some felt that the hardtop did not complement the lines as much. A steel sunroof was a popular option. These were intended as a limited-production vehicle, so the various panels were fitted to each car individually. As a result, these cars were substantially more expensive than the sedan version.

Fuel injection is worth the extra cost. It is somewhat easier to work with than the carburetors and they have a bit more power—115 brake horsepower at 4,800 rpm. Torque was also increased, to 152 foot-pounds at 4,100 rpm. Many 220SEs were equipped with the Hydrak clutch option.

These cars are more affordable than some of the other models and are becoming more popular among collectors and enthusiasts.

Behind the seats in this 190L is a storage area that lifts up and converts into a seat back and footwell for a passenger to sit side-saddle. This is something that could not be done with today's safety regulations.

The 220S strip speedometer shows the speed, and below are the various gauges for gas, oil, water, and electrics. A center-mounted clock is electric; the radio is directly below the clock. Above the glove box is a sculpted grab-handle for passengers. Completeness of the interior is important, because the trim bits are hard to find and are expensive.

With a total production run of approximately 1,942 cars over three years, the 220SE coupes and cabriolets are truly rare and collectible. The fit and finish of this 1960 coupe are spectacular.

Rust—Check for rust in and around the headlight and taillights. Both the nose and tail panels are susceptible to damage from rust or improper repairs. Pull and inspect headlights and taillights for signs of rust damage or repairs.

Chrome trim—It is everywhere on this car, and nowadays it is hard to find. Look for a car that has all the chrome (or as much as possible).

Trunk—Remove the mats in the trunk to check its condition and the presence of rust.

Floorboards—Pull interior carpeting to check their condition.

Appendix 1

Which Mercedes-Benz Do I Want?

Legend			
Body Style	**Description**	**Trans Type**	**Description**
Cpe	Coupe	4M	four-speed manual
Conv	Convertible	5M	five-speed manual
SL	Two-seat roadster	6M	six-speed manual
SLC	2+2	3A	three-speed automatic
HB	Three-door hatchback	4A	four-speed automatic
GW	Gullwing Coupe	5A	five-speed automatic
		6A	six-speed automatic
		7A	seven-speed automatic

Model Designation	Chassis Type	Years Mfg'd	Body Style	Engine Type	Cyl. Type	Trans
Section 1—SL/SLC/SLK						
230SL	113.042	'63–'67	SL	127.981	I-6	4M/4A
250SL	113.043	'66–'68	SL	127.982	I-6	4M/4A
280SL	113.044	'68–'71	SL	130.983	I-6	4M/5M/4A
350SL 4.5	107.043	'71–'73	SL	116.982	V-8	3A
350SLC 4.5	107.023	'71–'73	SLC	116.982	V-8	3A
450SL	107.044	'73–'75	SL	117.982	V-8	3A
450SL	107.044	'76–'80	SL	117.985	V-8	3A
450SLC	107.024	'73–'75	SLC	117.982	V-8	3A
450SLC	107.024	'76–'80	SLC	117.985	V-8	3A
380SL	107.045	'81–'82	SL	116.960	V-8	4A
380SL	107.045	'83–'85	SL	116.962	V-8	4A
560SL	107.048	'86–'89	SL	117.967	V-8	4A
300SL	129.061	'90–'93	SL	104.981	V-8	5M/5A
SL320	129.063	'94–'95	SL	104.991	V-8	5M/5A
500SL/SL500	129.067	'94–'02	SL	119.972	V-8	5A
600SL/SL600	129.076	'94–'02	SL	120.983	V-12	4A/5A
SLK230	170.447	'98–'00	SL	111.973	I-4	5A/5M
SLK230	170.449	'01–'04	SL	111.983	I-4	5A/5M/6M
SLK320	170.465	'02–'04	SL	112.947	V-6	5A/6M
SLK32 AMG	170.466	'02–'04	SL	112.960	V-6	5A
Section 2—Coupes/Convertibles						
220SEb	111.021	'60–'65	Cpe	127.984	I-6	4M/4A
220SEb	111.023	'60–'65	Conv	127.984	I-6	4M/4A
250SE	111.021	'65–'67	Cpe	129.980	I-6	4M/4A
250SE	111.023	'65–'67	Conv	129.980	I-6	4M/4A
300SE	112.023	'62–'63	Conv	189.958	I-6	4M/4A
300SE	112.021	'64–'67	Cpe	189.987	I-6	4M/4A
300SE	112.023	'64–'67	Conv	189.987	I-6	4M/4A
280SE	111.024	'67–'71	Cpe	130.980	I-6	4M/4A
280SE	111.025	'67–'71	Conv	130.980	I-6	4M/4A

Model Designation	Chassis Type	Years Mfg'd	Body Style	Engine Type	Cyl. Type	Trans
280SE 3.5	111.026	'69-'71	Cpe	116.980	V-8	4M/4A
280SE 3.5	111.027	'69-'71	Conv	116.980	V-8	4M/4A
250C	114.023	'69-'76	Cpe	114.923	I-6	4M/4A
280C	114.073	'72-'76	Cpe	110.921	I-6	4M/4A
280CE	123.053	'79-'81	Cpe	110.984	I-6	4A
300CD	123.150	'78-'81	Cpe	617.912	I-5	4A
300CD-Turbo	123.153	'81-'85	Cpe	617.952	I-5	4A
C230K 2.2L	203.747	'02	2Dr HB	111.975	I-4	5A/6M
C230K 1.8L	203.740	'03-present	2Dr HB	271.948	I-4	5A/6M
C320	203.764	'03-present	2Dr HB	112.946	V-6	5A/6M
300CE	124.050	'88-'89	Cpe	103.983	I-6	4A
300CE-24v	124.051	'90-'92	Cpe	104.980	I-6	4A
E320	124.052	'94-'95	Cpe	104.992	I-6	4A
E320	124.066	'94-'95	Conv	104.992	I-6	4A
CLK320	208.365	'98-'02	Cpe	112.940	V-6	5A
CLK320	208.465	'99-'03	Conv	112.940	V-6	5A
CLK430	208.370	'99-'02	Cpe	113.943	V-8	5A
CLK430	208.470	'00-'03	Conv	113.943	V-8	5A
CLK55 AMG	208.374	'01-'02	Cpe	113.984	V-8	5A
CLK55 AMG	208.474	'00-'03	Conv	113.984	V-8	5A
380SEC	126.043	'82-'83	Cpe	116.963	V-8	4A
500SEC	126.044	'84-'85	Cpe	117.963	V-8	4A
560SEC	126.045	'86-'91	Cpe	117.968	V-8	4A
500SEC	140.070	'93-'94	Cpe	119.970	V-8	4A/5A
S500	140.070	'95-'97	Cpe	119.970	V-8	4A/5A
CL500	140.070	'98-'99	Cpe	119.980	V-8	4A/5A
600SEC	140.076	'93-'94	Cpe	120.980	V-12	5A
S600	140.076	'95-'97	Cpe	120.980	V-12	5A
CL600	140.076	'98-'99	Cpe	120.982	V-12	5A
CL500	215.375	'00-present	Cpe	113.960	V-8	5A
CL55 AMG	215.373	'02	Cpe	113.986	V-8	5A
CL55 AMG	215.374	'03-present	Cpe	113.991	V-8	5A
CL600	215.378	'01-'02	Cpe	137.970	V-12	5A
CL600	215.376	'03-present	Cpe	275.950	V-12	5A

Section 3—Rare and Collectible

Model Designation	Chassis Type	Years Mfg'd	Body Style	Engine Type	Cyl. Type	Trans
300SL	198.040	'54-'57	GW	198.980	I-6	4M
300SL (alum)	198.043	'55-'56	GW	198.980	I-6	4M
300SL	198.042	'57-'63	SL	198.980	I-6	4M
190SL	121.040	'55-'61	Cpe	121.921	I-4	4M/AT
190SL	121.040	'61-'63	Cpe	121.928	I-4	4M/AT
190SL	121.042	'55-'61	SL	121.921	I-4	4M/AT
190SL	121.042	'61-'63	SL	121.928	I-4	4M/AT
220S	180.037	'57-'59	Cpe	180.924	I-6	4M
220S	180.030	'56-'59	Conv	180.924	I-6	4M
220SE	128.037	'58-'60	Cpe	127.984	I-6	4M
220SE	128.030	'58-'60	Conv	127.984	I-6	4M

Appendix 2
Mercedes-Benz Resources

There are many resources available to research any Mercedes-Benz that you may be interested in purchasing or simply learning more about. Listed here are some of the sites I frequently used in my search for additional knowledge about the cars.

Mercedes-Benz of America
www.mbusa.com

Mercedes-Benz Club of America
www.mbca.org

Mercedes-Benz related web pages and forums
www.benzworld.org

www.sportscarmarket.com
www.190slgroup.com
www.silverstarrestorations.com
www.slmarket.com
www.gullwinggroup.org
www.dearbornauto.com
www.hatchandsons.com
www.sportsleicht.com
www.dtemotorsports.com

www.paulrussell.com
www.oursl.com
www.roadfly.org/mercedes-benz/forums/
www.autobytel.com
www.carfax.com
www.consumerreports.org
www.edmunds.com
www.kbb.com
www.mesaperformance.com